Early praise for *The Way of the Web Tester*

The Way of the Web Tester is really *The Way of the Conscientious Web Developer*, providing a comprehensive journey through automated behavior-testing for web applications, from round-trip UI tests to fast-running unit tests. The examples are never simplistic, and helpful characters, including Diane the Developer and Tim the Tester, seem to know exactly what the reader is thinking. If you're writing web applications, you should have this book in your back pocket.

➤ **Dan North**
    Principal consultant, Dan North & Associates Ltd.

Everything in this book IS awesome! What I love most about *The Way of the Web Tester* is that it's a book for the whole team. Whether you're a tester nervous about coding skills, or a coder anxious about writing maintainable tests, this book will encourage you to collaborate for success. The step-by-step visuals will guide you through good coding and design practices and principles for robust, valuable automated tests. Most importantly, you'll learn how to deliver great software by writing tests first!

➤ **Lisa Crispin**
    Co-author with Janet Gregory of *More Agile Testing: Learning Journeys for the Whole Team*, www.agiletester.ca

This is a highly inspirational book on test automation: as a reader, you get a deep understanding of what role test automation plays and the value it brings for the tech industry. Whether you're a tester, developer, or product owner, after finishing there should no longer be any doubts: quality must be built in from the start.

➤ **Julia Oskö**
Engineer, Spotify

This book has some great ideas and examples, and I will recommend it to teams who are struggling with automation and how to start.

➤ **Janet Gregory**
Agile coach, with focus on testing, DragonFire Inc.

Chapter 1 is probably the best overview of automated testing I have ever read.

➤ **PJ Hampton**
PhD candidate and teaching assistant, Ulster University

The Way of the Web Tester

A Beginner's Guide to Automating Tests

Jonathan Rasmusson

The Pragmatic Bookshelf

Raleigh, North Carolina

Many of the designations used by manufacturers and sellers to distinguish their products are claimed as trademarks. Where those designations appear in this book, and The Pragmatic Programmers, LLC was aware of a trademark claim, the designations have been printed in initial capital letters or in all capitals. The Pragmatic Starter Kit, The Pragmatic Programmer, Pragmatic Programming, Pragmatic Bookshelf, PragProg and the linking *g* device are trademarks of The Pragmatic Programmers, LLC.

Every precaution was taken in the preparation of this book. However, the publisher assumes no responsibility for errors or omissions, or for damages that may result from the use of information (including program listings) contained herein.

Our Pragmatic books, screencasts, and audio books can help you and your team create better software and have more fun. Visit us at *https://pragprog.com*.

The yellow adhesive note graphic in Chapter 11 is designed by Layerace from Freepik.com.

The team that produced this book includes:

Development Editor: Susannah Davidson Pfalzer
Indexing: Potomac Indexing, LLC
Copy Editor: Nicole Abramowitz
Layout: Gilson Graphics
Producer: Janet Furlow

For sales, volume licensing, and support, please contact *support@pragprog.com*.

For international rights, please contact *rights@pragprog.com*.

Printed in the United States of America.
ISBN-13: 978-1-68050-183-4
Printed on acid-free paper.
Book version: P3.0—June 2017

Contents

Acknowledgements

This book would not have been possible were it not for the love of my life, Tannis, and our three wonderful children, Lucas, Rowan, and Brynn, who supported and loved me every step of the way.

A book like this doesn't happen without a wonderful editor and publisher. Everything quality can be attributed to Susannah Pfalzer. Everything else is mine.

And of course this book wouldn't be what it is without the incredible feedback and insight generously given by its reviewers and commenters:

Matteo Vaccari, Julia Oskö, Dan North, Kristian Karl, Fredrik Stridsman, Lisa Crispin, Michael Thelin, Bianca Mihai, Anders Ivarsson, Peter Hampton, Nigel Lowry, Javier Collado, Jason Yip, Elijah Wright, Michael Holland, Nicolae Ciocan, Loren Sands-Ramshaw, Rod Hilton, Gustav Hedberg, Colin Yates, Janet Gregory, Aisling Canton, Nouran Mhmoud, Jan Nonnen, Derek Graham, Kay Korper, Alexander Henry, Olivier Laguionie, Paul Waring, Lance Willett, Rachel Rosalia, and the wonderful people at Spotify.

Special thanks also to Nicole Abramowitz and Gilson Graphics for world-class copy editing and typesetting.

Thank you, Mom and Dad, for your love and encouragement.

And thanks to Dave and Andy for creating a company that lets aspiring authors create and share their work with the world.

It's Good to See You!

This is a book about how to write automated tests for the web. It's a book for anyone who has ever wanted to learn:

- How automated testing on the web works
- What the different kinds of automated tests are
- And, most importantly, how to get started writing them, even if you have little or no programming background or experience

Be warned—this isn't your typical deep dive tutorial book. We aren't going to spend hundreds of pages walking you through how to set up this kind of test framework or that. The technology changes too quickly.

Instead, we are going to focus on the fundamentals. Those things that simply don't change. These you will be able to take with you and apply to any project —regardless of which automated test framework or platform you choose to use.

And it is good to see you because automated testing is one of the greatest levers we've got for scaling the most valuable asset any software project has—you.

You see, you're kind of a big deal. We need more of you. We need more of your critical thinking. We need more of your creativity. And we need more of your time. And by learning how to write automated tests, that's really what you are giving yourself and the others on your team. More time.

If you are a traditional software tester who has little or no programming experience, this is the perfect book for getting started. Together we are going to start from the ground up and give you everything you need to create and start writing your very own automated tests today.

If you are a developer, but haven't thought a ton about how automated testing works, this is your crash course on how to move fast without breaking stuff. That means more time working on fun things, like adding new features, and less time working on the boring stuff, like fixing old bugs.

And if you are a team lead, this is your Rosetta Stone. This book will not only help you bridge the gap between traditional testers and developers, it will give you and your team the time, the language, and the framework to set your automated tests up right, while avoiding much of the duplication and wasted effort that usually comes to teams when they are just starting out.

How to Read This Book

If there are two chapters everyone on your team should read, they are Chapter 1, *The Testing Pyramid*, on page 3, and Chapter 8, *Climbing the Pyramid*, on page 125. These will give a nice overview of how automated testing works, along with the different kinds of tests and where and when to use each one.

For the rest of you, who actually want to know how this stuff works, the book is broken into two parts.

In Part I we go over the basics of how automated testing on the web works.

In Chapter 1, *The Testing Pyramid*, on page 3, we introduce the concept of the testing pyramid: a model all teams can use to coordinate their testing efforts and ensure we are all on the same page.

In Chapter 2, *Smoking User Interface Tests*, on page 19, we introduce the concept of the user interface (UI) test and see how this test helps us test our systems just like a regular user would. And in Chapter 3, *Adding UI Tests to Legacy Systems*, on page 33, we put the theory into practice and see what it takes to add UI tests to an existing legacy system.

In Chapter 4, *Connecting the Dots with Integration Tests*, on page 53, we then dive deeper into the world of the web and see how to test web services directly. We then apply that knowledge in Chapter 5, *Integration Testing RESTful Web Services*, on page 67, where we see how to test what is arguably the most popular kind of web API out there today: RESTful web services.

In Chapter 6, *Covering Our Bases with Unit Tests*, on page 79, we see why unit tests play such an important role in test automation today. And, specifically, we explore how to unit test JavaScript in the browser in Chapter 7, *Unit Testing in the Browser with JavaScript*, on page 99.

And in Chapter 8, *Climbing the Pyramid*, on page 125, we bring it all together and see how the pyramid works in action, starting at the top and then working our way down to the bottom, highlighting a few of the challenges you're likely to meet along the way.

In Part II we move beyond the basics and get into some of the more advanced topics that come with the territory.

In Chapter 9, *Programming 101*, on page 139, we look at the techniques programmers use to write good code, and see how to adapt those strategies for writing good tests.

In Chapter 10, *Organizing Tests:*, on page 163, we take a look at all those tests you're going to write, and see how we can go about organizing them in a nice and easy way.

In Chapter 11, *Effective Mocking*, on page 179, we look at some of the pitfalls developers can fall into when relying heavily on mocks and how to avoid them.

And in Chapter 12, *Writing Tests First*, on page 199, we see what writing tests first is like, and how it can help us deal with the complexity and design challenges we face when writing our very first tests.

A Few Conventions

One of the trickier things about writing a book like this is choosing the computer language to do the examples in. I picked Ruby, along with its sidekick Ruby on Rails, and JavaScript for a couple of reasons.

Ruby was chosen because there is a lot to be learned from this community about automated testing and web development in general. That, and Ruby is a fairly easy language to understand and learn—even if you aren't a programmer.

JavaScript is in here because so much of the web is powered by it today. We have an entire chapter dedicated to how it can be used to test functionality in the browser.

But this shouldn't be viewed as an authoritative book on JavaScript or Ruby. These are simply the tools we use today.

Much more important are the fundamentals. Things like HTML, CSS, and HTTP. So we are going to spend more time on these, and less on any particular tool or framework.

The goal here is for you to get so good at the fundamentals that the frameworks and tools they are built upon won't matter.

Fun Bits with Purpose

You can't take this stuff too seriously, and it helps if you can approach the material with a sense of humor.

To that end, I've tried to lighten things up with pictures, stories, and anecdotes to share with you along the way.

War stories are real-life, from-the-trenches experiences about some of the successes and failures I and others have had while writing automated tests. You'll know it's a war story when you see the archer.

The Now You Try exercises are there to snap you out of reading and get you into thinking and doing. So keep a pen or pencil handy.

 This means you get to think and write!

Then there are Tim and Diane—our traditional tester and developer. Tim and Diane don't have a lot of experience when it comes to automated testing. But what they lack in experience, they more than make up for in enthusiasm and questions.

I'VE NEVER AUTOMATED A TEST BEFORE IN MY LIFE !

Tim the Tester

I AM TIRED OF FIXING OLD BUGS !

Diane the Developer

And when you see a thumb, get ready for a timely tip or piece of advice.

 Write good automated tests so you will have
more time to do exploratory testing.

Online Resources

You can always reach me, or just send feedback on how the book could be better, at the book's web page, pragprog.com/book/jrtest. Here you can find source code, ask questions, report bugs, and generally discuss all things book related. Make sure you drop by and say hi.

Alright. Let's begin.

Part I

Mapping the Pyramid

The testing pyramid is the model we use to describe the various kinds of automated tests we typically see on projects. In this part, we are going to look at three kinds of automated tests and develop some rules of thumb around where and when to use each one.

The Testing Pyramid

What kind of test should we write?

Before we can talk automated testing, we need to lay down some groundwork. In this chapter, we set up the framework, model, and language we're going to use to discuss automated testing for the rest of the book. Something called the *testing pyramid*.

Learning the pyramid will not only make you more knowledgeable in automated testing, it will give you a feel for how each kind of test works, along with how they fit together and complement one another.

This will give you the vocabulary to talk automated testing along with the insight to know where and how to use each kind of test.

It Was Beautiful

The year was 2001, and my team and I were feeling rather proud of ourselves. We had just put the finishing touches on what we thought was the Rolls-Royce of automated testing tools. We had built our very own, homegrown, fully automated, UI testing framework. And it was amazing!

This thing had everything. With the click of a button, you could fire up the app, record a test, and then play it back while making assertions about things you had seen along the way. It was easy to use. Running the tests made for great demos (because you could actually see the application running). And the best part of all, our build engineers had even found a way to include the scripts as part of our continuous build and integration process—meaning we would know instantly if something had broken.

It was a masterpiece of human ingenuity.

We loved it. Our testers loved it. Our customers loved it. And everything was great. Until...

The Wheels on the Bus

It didn't happen all at once. It kind of snuck up on us slowly at first. But we eventually began to notice that the more we used our automated testing framework, the harder it got to add new features to the system.

At first it wasn't immediately clear why. We had good automated test coverage. We were continuously integrating our changes and regularly releasing the software to clients. We saw no reasons why writing lots of automated UI tests like this should slow us down. But when we dug a little deeper, we discovered a few disturbing trends.

First off, developers had stopped writing a certain kind of automated test called a *unit test*. These tests were fast, little code-based tests that we relied on to tell us quickly if anything was ever broken in the software. By not writing those, and instead replacing them with longer-running user interface tests, our automated builds took longer to run. Which meant we didn't know till much later which changes broke which tests.

This in turn created another problem. Because the tests were now taking longer to run, developers stopped running them. Many started ignoring them altogether. We had deadlines after all, and builds that used to take ten minutes were now taking upwards of three hours. No one had time to wait for a three-hour build. So the build was perpetually broken. And even worse, people started checking in new code on top of it.

Then one day it all came to a head. We missed a critical deadline. We were stuck. There were tons of bugs in the software. We couldn't easily add any new functionality. And for the first time, we had to confront the uncomfortable truth that our beloved test framework was the source of many of our problems.

What happened? How had something that started out so good morphed into something that ended up hurting so bad?

Three Hard Lessons Learned

While it didn't feel particularly good at the time, this project taught us some valuable lessons about test automation:

1. Not all automated tests are created equal. Some tests are better at testing certain things than others.

2. Just because you can write a certain kind of automated test doesn't necessarily mean you should.

3. Speed and feedback matter. The longer it takes your test cases to run, the slower and less iterative your development cycle.

What we and others were learning from these experiences was that automated testing wasn't a one-size-fits-all thing. There were different kinds of tests, and each tested different kinds of things.

Fortunately, others were feeling the same pain we were. And eventually, some of these learnings started to form as pictures and models in people's minds. And one very useful one that slowly emerged was called the *testing pyramid*.

Enter the Testing Pyramid

The testing pyramid, first coined by Mike Cohn in *Succeeding with Agile* [Coh09], is a model that teams use to show how three different kinds of tests complement each other.

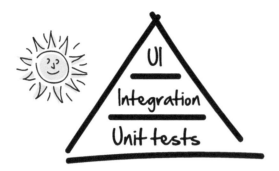

At the top of the pyramid, we've got these things called *user interface* or *UI tests*. These tests go end-to-end through the entire system and act just like a user would if they were using the system. We'll cover UI tests in Chapter 2, *Smoking User Interface Tests*, on page 19.

Then we've got *integration tests*. These are like UI tests, except they don't go through the user interface. They instead go one layer beneath and directly test the underlying services that make our user interfaces go. We cover these in Chapter 4, *Connecting the Dots with Integration Tests*, on page 53.

Then at the base we've got these things called *unit tests*: small, fast, precise code-level tests developers write to tell instantly when things are broken. These come later, in Chapter 6, *Covering Our Bases with Unit Tests*, on page 79.

Chapter Ordering

Now when it comes to exploring the pyramid, we're going to start at the top with the UI tests and then work our way down to the bottom. We're going to do this for three reasons:

1. Quick wins.

    UI tests are the easiest of the three types of tests to get going with, and scoring some quick wins will put some wind in our sails and make tackling the subsequent chapters easier.

2. We need some basics.

    The chapter on JavaScript won't make sense until you understand a few mechanics about how HTML and CSS work. So we are going to cover those first in Chapter 2, *Smoking User Interface Tests*, on page 19.

3. Sticky learning.

    Over the course of the book, I am going to occasionally lead you down some garden paths and show you how some things seem great, only to then show you where they fail. This will give you a better feel for what each type of test can do, along with where their limits lie.

So don't think of the chapter ordering as showing the levels of importance—most teams start with unit tests first. But we are starting at the top to aid with learning, which will hopefully make the material more sticky and fun along the way.

Three Levels

The testing pyramid makes more sense once you understand that most web software architectures are made up of three distinct layers.

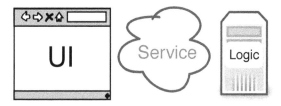

There's a UI layer, which contains the buttons and controls your customers use when using your application. There's the *service layer*, which feeds your UI layer the data it needs to update its displays. And then there is the *logic layer*, which contains the math, calculations, and brains of the operation.

Now of course not every application is built this way. Some have business logic built into the service layer. Some applications don't have any UI. These differences don't usually matter. The fundamentals of the pyramid still tend to hold.

What matters is understanding that each layer of these applications maps to a specific level in our pyramid, and that each level has a certain kind of test.

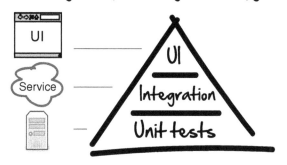

Let's take a quick look at each of these layers now.

UI Tests

The user interface tests test the application from the UI layer down.

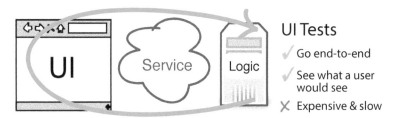

This is what makes UI tests so desirable. They cut through all the layers of the architecture and ensure everything is hooked up. That's what we mean when we say UI tests go *end-to-end*.

The downside to this end-to-end awesomeness is speed and fragility. UI tests tend to be slow and fragile. UI tests don't have to be brittle (we'll look at some ways to make them more robust in Chapter 2, *Smoking User Interface Tests*, on page 19). But there's no getting around the fact that they are slow—orders of magnitude slower than unit tests. So they are not the greatest for giving rapid feedback. This is why UI tests sit at the top of the pyramid and tend to be used more sparingly on projects.

Integration Tests

Integration tests, on the other hand, don't go through the UI. They start one layer down and test the underlying services. This gives them the advantage of not having to deal with the fragility of the UI, while still retaining some of the ability to check that things are properly hooked up and connected.

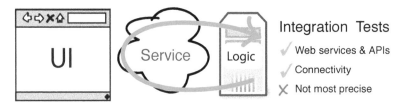

The only downside to integration tests is that they aren't very precise. By precise, I mean that while they are great at telling you something is broken, they can't always tell you exactly where.

So we like integration tests, because they are great at testing connectivity, but we still don't use them for everything because they can't always tell us exactly where our problems lie.

Unit Tests

For precision, speed, and coverage, we rely on unit tests. Unit tests are the granddaddy of all automated tests. Developers started writing these things years ago with the rise of agile methods like extreme programming,[1] and they have become a staple in modern programming languages and platforms.

They are extremely quick and very precise. And when things break, they tell us exactly where things went wrong. They are essential for rapid iterative development, and without these, we would be flying blind.

The only downside to all that speed and precision is integration. Sometimes unit tests miss things. Certain bugs only appear when we hook things up. This is why integration tests are still so valuable. And why developers will typically write both when testing their systems.

When we bring all these tests together, some rules of thumb start to form.

Rules of Thumb

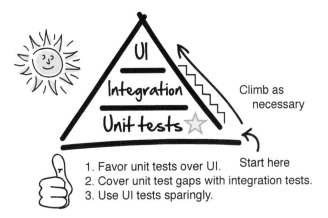

1. Favor unit tests over UI.
2. Cover unit test gaps with integration tests.
3. Use UI tests sparingly.

---

1.   http://www.agilenutshell.com/xp

The pyramid takes its shape from experience, which has taught us that it is better to do the bulk of our automated testing down near the bottom, where the tests are fast and cheap, than at the top where they are slow and expensive.

Not all projects have or need end-to-end UI-style tests. Some get by with just unit and integration.

That's why whenever we go and add new tests to the system, we always start at the bottom first, and work our way up from there.

When adding a new test, always see if you can cover it with a unit test first.

Now if you're a tester, this is hard advice to follow because you won't be automating things near the bottom. You will instead be working with the higher-level tests closer to the top. So the flip side of this for you is to:

Always push tests as far down the pyramid as you can.

That means if you can handle a given test case with an integration test, that's favorable to trying to automate everything up in the UI.

And this final rule of thumb takes a moment to say but a lifetime to master:

Don't try to automate everything. Instead automate just enough.

As wonderful as automated tests are, every test has a price in terms of cost and maintenance. So we don't want to automate everything. Instead we want to automate just enough. Easy to say—hard to do. We will explore this Zen-like principle more as we get further into the book.

Some overlap of tests in terms of functionality is inevitable, because tests near the top are always going to be supersets of those near the bottom.

Tests near the top wrap those near the bottom ...

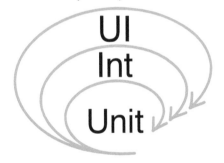

but they differ in terms of scope and intent.

For example, we might have a unit test that verifies that passwords need to be at least eight characters in length, while any UI test that logs in will inadvertently end up testing the same thing too. So there's no avoiding that.

What we can avoid, however, is blatant duplication. We never want to write the exact same tests between different layers of the pyramid because that would be wasteful. If we know we've got some scenario covered at the unit test level, there's no sense in duplicating it directly up top in the UI.

If it helps, think of the difference between UI and unit tests like this.

Unit tests vs UI tests

are about development	are about verification
rapid feedback	slow feedback
very low level	very high level
very local	go end-to-end
cheap	expensive
fast	slow
solid	fragile
reliable / deterministic	flaky / non-deterministic
used to develop	used to test
test from developer's POV	test from customer's POV

UI and integration tests are about connectivity. It's OK for those tests to be slower because they go through more layers of the architecture. That's why we love them! They are making sure things work end-to-end.

Unit tests, on the other hand, are about speed and feedback. We write unit tests when we are looking for feedback about things that are important to us during development. Things like:

- Did we get our design right?
- Did we break anything with the last set of changes?
- Do all our assumptions and edge cases check out?
- Is it safe to add new functionality?

Unit tests are what enable us to iterate quickly. UI and integration tests are about making sure things work end-to-end. Both serve an important purpose. They're just two different sides of the same coin.

So yes, some duplication in functionality is perfectly fine, just so long as we are not duplicating intent.

And that's basically it! That's the pyramid. The rest of the book is just going to focus on the details of where and when to write each of these tests, and show you how they work in the real world for the web.

But that does leave us with one interesting question. If you are on a mixed team made up of developers and testers, who exactly should be writing these things?

Who's Writing These Things

One of the interesting challenges with multi-disciplinary teams is figuring out who's doing what. Especially now that quality is a team responsibility.

Because not only does testing now blend what has been two traditional separate camps in software (development and testing), we now get to deal with all the different words, meanings, and sometimes even different philosophies that go into the purpose of automated testing itself!

Devs — Conflicting philosophies — QA

Devs	QA
speed	correctness
development	verification
offense	defense
enabling change	playing it safe
test what's required	test everything

around the purpose of automated testing

For example, for devs, automated testing is all about speed. Automated tests (specifically unit tests) are what enable developers to move fast without breaking stuff. Unit tests run quickly. They tell the developers when they've broken stuff in the code. And they are what allow developers to make changes fearlessly. So slow, long-running tests are no good for developers. All they are looking for is rapid feedback and speed.

Traditional testers, on the other hand, are more worried about correctness. We've traditionally put so much pressure on testers to be thorough and to catch every possible bug, that to a traditional tester, testing is all about thoroughness, breadth, and depth. To them, the more automated tests the better—regardless of how fast or how long it takes them to run.

And therein lies the rub. You've got two conflicting, competing forces already at play around the very purpose of automated testing, and you haven't even started your project.

This is why so many automated testing initiatives invariably start off looking something like this.

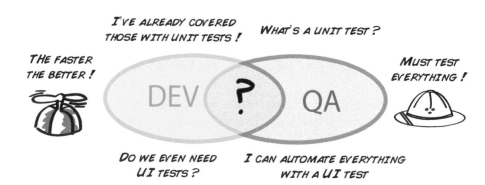

Conflict. You've got different definitions of success. Different definitions of tests. And a lot of confusion around who should be doing what when it comes to these things called automated tests.

While there are no hard and fast rules about who does what, I've seen a couple of different ways to make this work.

Testers typically work at the upper levels of the pyramid—specifically the UI and integration layers. These tests tend to line up nicely with the kind of work traditional testers are usually already doing: end-to-end system testing. If you are a traditional tester, it's natural to start up here.

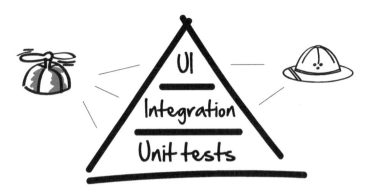

Developers, on the other hand, are really into unit tests. Sure they can, and often do, test at all levels of the pyramid. But there is usually so much automated testing work to be done, most are more than happy to have others chip in and help out. They often work across all three, supporting testers at the upper levels and helping set up the necessary tests and infrastructure needed to get the testers going.

Developers today also realize that having a full-time dedicated tester on a team is a luxury, and that the days of having others take responsibility for the quality of their work are long gone. They are responsible for the quality of their code—no one else.

However you and your team decide to do it, collaboration and pairing is key. You want to avoid testers doing one thing at the top of the pyramid, oblivious to what developers are doing at the bottom. That's where all the waste and duplicated effort usually sneaks in.

If you're a tester, you want to be joined at the hip with your developer so you can coordinate which kinds of automated tests you each want to write. In the beginning, it may be the developer doing most of the setup (it's always good to get a few good examples going). But after that, there's no reason why you can't jump in there and start taking on more test automation responsibility.

And if you're a developer, it's in your best interests to make your testers as productive as possible, because the less time they have to spend retesting things that can readily be automated, the more time you'll both have for exploratory testing—which is where the magic really happens. So pair with your testers, teach them how to write their own automated tests, and coordinate your actions with theirs. You'll get better coverage and fewer bugs.

Regardless of what you and your team decide, know there is almost always more automated testing to be done on any given project than time and resources will allow. That's why you gotta automate smart.

At the end of the day, don't worry so much about who's doing what. What's more important is that it gets done, and the people getting it done are most often those with the passion and drive to make it happen. You don't need to have any fancy title or role for that.

Don't Forget About Exploratory Testing

With all this automated testing going on, it's easy to forget another important kind of testing we always want to make sure we are doing on projects: exploratory testing.

Exploratory testing is just what the label says: unscripted, exploratory testing where you systematically go through the application and try to break it.

It's a powerful testing technique, because unlike the scripted tests, exploratory testing is our chance to uncover things that simply don't show up in automated tests.

Automated testing is a means to enable us to do more exploratory testing. So once you've got a good suite of automated tests, don't forget to go back and continuously explore.

Read *Explore It! [Hen13]* by Elisabeth Hendrickson for a great book on exploratory testing.

What We've Learned So Far

Congratulations! You now know more about automated testing than most, and you are all set for the next time the testing pyramid comes up as a conversation starter at your next cocktail party.

Here's a quick recap of what we've covered so far:

- We typically write three kinds of automation tests on projects: UI, integration, and unit.

- When adding a new test, see if you can cover it with a unit test first.

- Always push tests down the pyramid as far as you can.

- Avoid waste and duplication by collaborating with your team at all levels of the pyramid.

This is a good first step. We now have some common language and some shared vocabulary to talk about automated testing.

In the next chapter on UI testing, we are going to jump right in and see what UI tests are, and the critical role they play in making sure the important stuff always works. Let's go!

CHAPTER 2

Smoking User Interface Tests

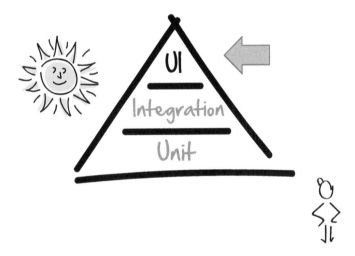

In this chapter, we take a look at how to write the most complete end-to-end test in our automated testing arsenal: the user interface test.

Learning how to write good UI tests will not only ensure key features of your software are always up and running, but it will free you to spend more time on the more tricky parts of your software that need your attention most—like exploratory testing.

Testers, this is a good chapter for you because you definitely have a role to play in helping write good UI tests. And developers, this chapter will help you understand the mechanics behind how these automated UI test frameworks work, so you can ultimately make your applications more testable.

By the end of this chapter, you'll know what UI tests are and how they work, and you'll have one super handy tool for ensuring key pieces of your system are always up and running.

Another Botched Release

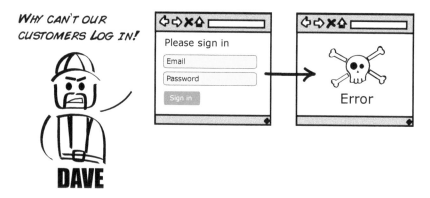

Dave the construction manager is normally a mild-mannered guy. But today he's upset. Dave is mad because for the second time this month, the login page to his work permit system has broken. That means construction engineers can't log in. They can't get their work permits. Which means they can't legally work. And Dave wants to know why!

Normally we would have run a set of manual QA scripts before pushing things out, but Suzy was on holiday and no one told the developers we were pushing things out a day early because of the holiday.

Obviously, we've got some communication problems, but isn't there something we can do, right now, to ensure this never happens again? Some kind of script, or test thingy, that could just log in to the system, try some things out, and report back if there were any errors?

Enter the User Interface Test

User interface tests (or UI tests) are scripts that test your application in the same way an end user would. They click, tap, select, log in, and do things you or I would, which is why they are so handy.

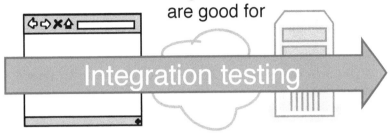

What makes UI tests nice is that they slice through all the layers of the application and go end-to-end. End-to-end means exercising all the different parts of the application—the user interface, the underlying services, all the way to the database. This is what makes UI tests so good at testing connectivity, which is why we often use them as high-level smoke tests.

Smoke tests are super high-level tests that verify that at some basic level our system is up and running. They are handy because they tell us if

- Our applications are correctly deployed
- Our environments are correctly configured
- All the pieces of our architecture are connected and hooked up right

The term *smoke test* comes from the older days when if you wanted to see if an electrical device was working, you could plug it into the wall and look for smoke. If you saw any, that was bad.

But we like smoke tests because they guarantee that at some minimal level our systems are always working. Which is why they make great UI tests.

Take logging in, for example. If we were to write a UI test for logging in, what steps would our test need to go through to verify that someone could enter their credentials, log into the system, and then be redirected to the Welcome page?

Take a minute and see if you can write out in plain English the steps necessary to do this yourself. Bonus points if you figure out what we should assert at the end of our test.

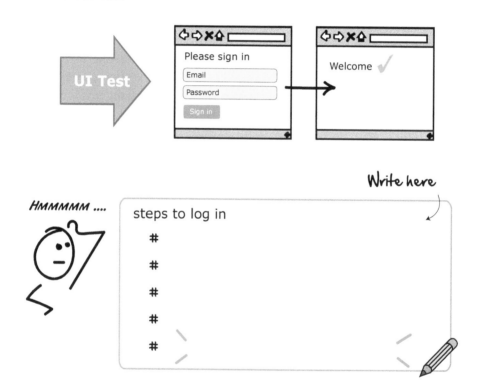

Were you able to write out the basic steps? This is what we generally do when writing UI tests. We think about what we would do as a user, and then write that script out in the form of a test. Here's one way we could go about automating this.

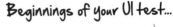

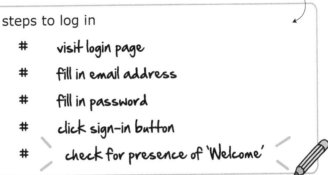

First we would have to navigate to the login page. Once there we could fill out our email address and password. Next we would need to log in by clicking the sign-in button. And then we would want to check and see that we somehow got redirected to the Welcome page.

Once we've got our script, it's simply a matter of converting it into some kind of test. Something like this:

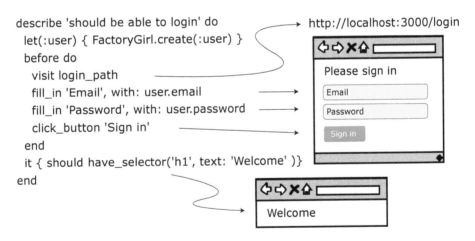

Now this is our first automated test, so don't worry if you don't understand everything going on here at first glance. We are going to walk every line of this test shortly.

Also, remember we are just getting our feet wet here with the basics in this book, and you can always find more advanced, technical tutorial books on the subject of how to set these tests up.

We are just using Rails here as an example. The principles we are about to uncover will work just as well for any other testing/development framework of your choice.

Now this test is written in Ruby using a library called RSpec. And the way RSpec describes the names of its tests is that it puts the test name in quotes, between those describe and do keywords. In this case, we are saying the name of this test will be should be able to login.

```
describe 'should be able to login' do
```

The next line creates a fake test user for us.

```
let(:user) { FactoryGirl.create(:user) }
```

We can't log in without a user. And this line here, using a Rails gem called FactoryGirl, creates one for us. Gem is another word for library in Ruby, so if you hear the word *gem*, just think *library*. All this line of code does is give us access to a fake, but valid, user that we can access for a username and password in our test.

With that setup done, we are now ready to visit the login page. The way we get there in our tests is with this line here:

```
visit login_path
```

This line does pretty much what it says. It visits the login page by navigating to the login page's URL. In Rails, that is conveniently defined for us in a variable called login_path. This variable actually maps to the URL http://localhost:3000/login.

 Use variables to describe commonly used URLs in your test cases.

Rails does this so you don't have to remember and type that login URL string every time you want to use it. Having variables also makes our tests easier to read, so you will want to use variables in your tests whenever you can.

These three lines you can probably figure out:

```
fill_in 'Email', with: user.email
fill_in 'Password', with: user.password
click_button 'Sign in'
```

The first two use that fake user we created earlier and fill its username and password into their respective text boxes. And the third line there selects and clicks the sign-in button.

See how easy that reads? Here we are literally *filling in* the email and password text boxes with some valid user credentials.

After that, it's simply one line to check and see that we got redirected to the Welcome page correctly. We can be sure that we have, if we can find an HTML H1 header containing the text *Welcome*.

```
it { should have_selector('h1', text: 'Welcome' )}
```

Congratulations! You've just walked through your first UI test. Well done!

Now that may not have looked too bad, but believe it or not, there was a lot of magic going on behind the scenes to make all that happen.

Let's now dive a little deeper and see how those UI test frameworks made grabbing those page elements look so easy, as well as how they know which page elements we were looking for.

Say No to Record/Playback

With all these automated user interactions going on, you'd think capturing UI tests with record/playback tools would be a good thing. It usually isn't. Here's why.

Tests generated from record/playback tools tend to be brittle and fragile. Change one little thing in the UI and boom! Your tests break.

Second, record/playbacks are highly unreadable. The tests these tools create may be fine for machines, but they are practically unreadable to us humans.

And third, when we use record/playback, we give up the most powerful tool we have for organizing our tests—writing them in code. Code is wonderful because when we write tests in code, we get to do amazing things.

We can write reusable components. We have full control over what happens. And we can see and understand exactly what's going on. We give all that up when we go record/playback.

It's OK to use record/playback just to experiment, learn, and see how things are going. But when it comes to writing production-ready tests, do yourself a favor and set the record/playback aside. It may take you somewhere fast, but it's going to take you and your tests in the wrong direction.

How They Work

Imagine for a second you are a UI test framework, and an automated tester was asking you to grab certain page elements that they wanted to interact with. How would you do it?

Would you search for some matching text? Would you try to grab elements by their type? Or perhaps would you look for some kind of unique identifier separating one particular element from all the others?

Believe it or not, UI testing frameworks do all those things. And they do it on the web by relying on two key technologies: HTML and CSS.

HTML Is for Asserting

HTML (HyperText Markup Language) is the markup language we use to describe the content in our web pages. What do we mean by *describe*? Well, when we view things in our browser, we need to describe what it is we are seeing.

For example, say we wanted to create a page containing a heading, an image of an apple, and a sentence. We could do all that in HTML like this.

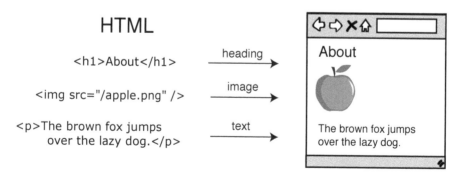

Those funny things in brackets you see (<h1>, <img>, and <p>) are called *tags*. And when we put those things around the content we want to describe, we *mark it up*.

Now these tags are important because they are what our UI testing frameworks look for when we write our automated UI tests.

So when we ask our UI testing framework to make assertions (statements that are either true or false) about what content should or should not appear on the page, or to verify the presence of some control, we use these tags to tell it what we are talking about.

But in order to get our hands on those tags, we first need to select them. And for that we have CSS.

CSS Is for Selecting

CSS (Cascading Style Sheets), like HTML, is another markup language. But instead of marking up content, with CSS we mark up style.

For example, let's say we want to add a little polish to the content of our web page, and style the page using a nice-looking footer, a header, and a main content area. The content we would leave in the HTML, but styling we would put in the CSS.

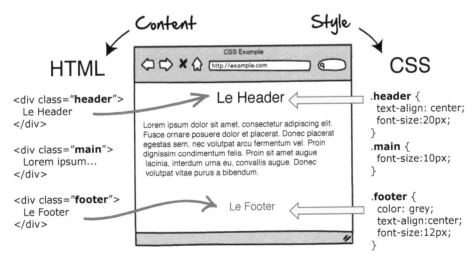

CSS is what gives our web pages their look and feel. It handles the alignment of our page elements. It gives us the size and color of our text. CSS also has one other unique property that we rely on heavily for UI tests—its ability to select page elements.

By using these things called CSS selectors, we can grab page elements we want to manipulate in our tests, and get them to do things just like our users would as if they were using the system.

For example, say we wanted to grab all the text input fields on a given web page. We could do that with a CSS selector that looks something like this.

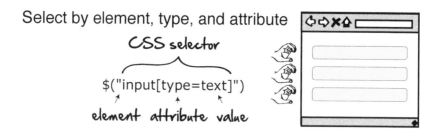

Now this syntax may look a little strange at first. That $() syntax is a shortcut browsers use[1] to save us some typing when we want to query a page for all the elements matching a given CSS selector.

$( ) ⟶ document.querySelector( )

The stuff we are interested in is what goes inside the $()—namely, the selector.

The way to read the preceding selector goes something like this:

Give me all the input page elements with attribute type text.

---

1. https://developers.google.com/web/tools/chrome-devtools/debug/command-line/expressions?hl=en#select-elements

And when you run this selector against a web page, that's exactly what it will do. It will return us all page elements of type text.

Why Isn't My CSS Working?

If for some reason your CSS selectors aren't grabbing anything, try replacing

```
$("")
```

with

```
document.querySelector("")
```

$() is jQuery shorthand for "get me this element." jQuery is a popular JavaScript library that many websites use. But if you run into a website that doesn't seem to want to select anything, try using the longer, more formal way of selecting page elements.

So, document.querySelector("#user_name") instead of $("#user_name"). It may be what's tripping things up.

Now grabbing multiple text boxes is fine (this is normally what we want when styling web pages with CSS). But when writing UI tests, we usually want just one page element: the one we are interacting with.

One way to grab a specific page element in CSS is to modify our CSS slightly and grab an element by its position.

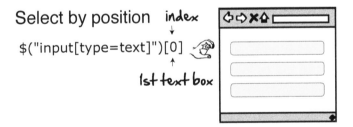

This might also look a little strange. First off, the results that come back to us are in the form of an array (those things in square brackets containing a 0). What's also weird is that the first element of that array starts with a 0.

Array elements starting with 0 is a convention that caught on early in computer programming. It has to do with keeping the math simple when allocating computer memory (it was easier to start the counting at 0 instead of 1). Anyways, it became a convention and now pretty much all computer languages use this as the standard way to grab the first element of an array—in our case, the first input field text box.

Now grabbing elements by their position works, but you need to be careful.

 Be careful when grabbing UI elements by their position.

If you write UI tests that are dependent on an element's relative position, what do you think will happen as soon as someone changes the layout of your page?

Boom! Your tests will break because the elements (and their indexes) are no longer in the same position. This is one reason why UI tests are so fragile.

So to avoid this, the preferred way to grab UI elements is to select them with something that uniquely identifies them. In the case of the web, it's by their *IDs*.

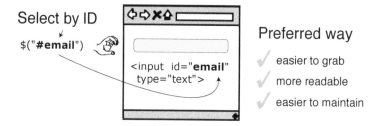

By adding ID attributes to the elements you want to select, selecting your page elements gets a whole lot easier.

By doing this, you guarantee that one—and only one—page element should ever return for a given match. Because you get to choose the name of the ID yourself, you can give it a nice easy-to-understand name, simultaneously making your test easier to read and understand.

And that is how UI testing frameworks in general work. You give unique identifiers to the elements you want to select, and then grab them according to some selection criteria. For the web, that's CSS selectors.

What We've Learned So Far

Are you still with me? I know a lot of this stuff can seem a little abstract and weird at first, but now that we've got some of the theory out of the way, we are in a good position because things are going to get very real shortly.

Here's a quick recap of the important stuff from this chapter:

• UI tests make for great end-to-end smoke tests.

- We prefer tests written in code over record/playback scripts.
- HTML is what we look for when we are making assertions in our tests.
- CSS selectors are how we select page elements we want to grab.
- Page elements are easier to grab when they are decorated with unique HTML IDs.

Now it's time to put some of this theory into practice and see what it is like to add automated UI tests for a legacy system. Which is exactly what Dave would like us to do for him right now.

CHAPTER 3

Adding UI Tests to Legacy Systems

Dave has another older legacy page that's been acting up lately: his customer sign-up page.

At first glance, this page looks pretty similar to our login page. But when we try writing a similar-looking UI test for it like we did with our login page, it fails!

cswp/spec/requests/user_pages_spec.rb

```ruby
describe 'When creating a new user' do

  subject { page }

  describe 'with valid credentials' do

    before do
      # create a new user
      visit signup_path
      fill_in 'Name', with: 'New User'
      fill_in 'Email', with: 'user@example.com'
      fill_in 'Password', with: 'foobar'
      fill_in 'Confirmation', with: 'foobar'
      click_button 'Create my account'
    end
```

```ruby
describe 'after saving the user' do
  # find the new user we just created
  let(:user) { User.find_by(email: 'user@example.com') }

  # make some assertions
  it { should have_content(user.name) }
  it { should have_selector('.alert-success') }
end
```
```
  end
end
```

For some reason, the tests and selectors we used in the previous login page test don't work here. And when we try running it, we get error messages saying things like, "Unable to find fields Name, Email, and Password."

To see why, let's write this test from scratch and take a look at what's going on under the hood of this web page. And while doing this, let's also look at some useful techniques for writing UI tests from scratch.

Step 1: Confirm You're on the Right Test Page

Before doing anything fancy in a test, it's always good to confirm you're testing the right page. I know, this sounds obvious. But you'd be surprised how much time you can waste thinking you're testing one page, when you are inadvertently testing another.

The easiest way to verify you're hitting the right page is simply to navigate to it in your test, and then print out the HTML response that comes back.

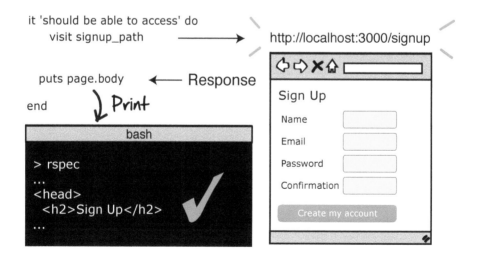

We haven't covered the basics yet around how HTTP requests and responses work (hang in there, we'll do this shortly in Chapter 4, *Connecting the Dots with Integration Tests*, on page 53). But all we are doing here is connecting to a web page and then printing out its contents.

If you see some HTML that looks familiar (that is, it contains the headers and text fields you're looking for), you'll know you are in the right place. If you don't, well then, give yourself a pat on the back—you've discovered the first bug in your test!

Printing out HTML responses from test frameworks is usually pretty straightforward. We first need to get our hands on the web server response, and we need to print it out. Usually by doing something like this:

Language	Print command
Ruby	puts "hello"
Java	System.out.println("hello");
Python	print("hello");
JavaScript	console.log("hello");
C#	Console.WriteLine("hello");
Objective-C	NSLog("Welcome");

Once we're confident we are in the right place, we can then get to work on our selectors.

Step 2: Figure Out Your CSS Selectors

Before you can make anything happen in a UI test, you need to get your hands on the controls you want to manipulate. For us, that means the four input fields capturing the user account details, as well as the sign-in button that triggers the form submission.

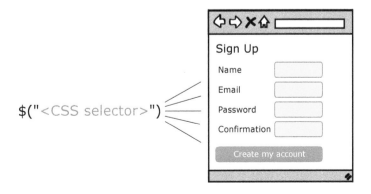

For web pages, that means looking at the underlying HTML and then seeing what CSS selectors we can write to grab them.

One way to do this is to open up your favorite browser (the following examples use Google Chrome), navigate to the page under test, right-click anywhere on the page, and select the *View Page Source* option.

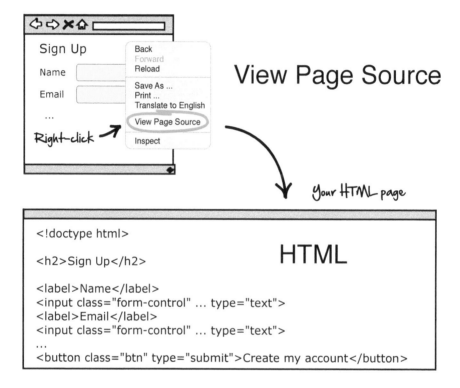

View Page Source shows us the underlying HTML of all the controls on the page, as well everything else that went into this page's construction.

Now what's interesting about this legacy page is that when we look at the controls we're trying to select, we immediately see why our earlier test didn't work. The page elements we were trying to select don't have any IDs!

No wonder we couldn't grab those controls. Our test framework was expecting our controls to be uniquely identified with IDs like name, email, and password, but by not having them, our framework couldn't grab them.

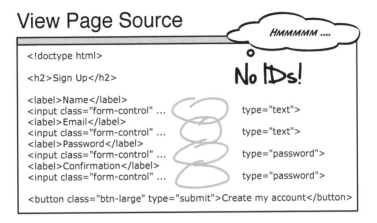

Not having IDs on our elements isn't the end of the world. But it certainly makes grabbing the controls harder.

Using IDs has a number of advantages. For one, it makes our CSS selectors way easier to write—all we need are the IDs of the controls we want to manipulate and we're done. But secondly, it makes our tests easier to read because well-named IDs are much less cryptic than plain old CSS.

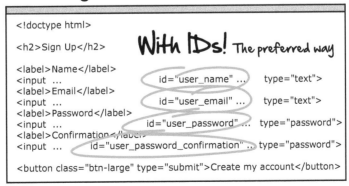

Some Test Frameworks Have Built-In Affordances

One thing test frameworks sometimes do to make our testing lives easier is give us convenience routines, or affordances, to make the selecting of page elements easier.

For example, did you notice how the login page UI test was able to use Name as a selecting field?

```
fill_in 'Name', with: 'New User'
```

But our customer sign-in page had to use user_name?

```
fill_in 'user_name', with: 'New User'
```

That's because in the login page test, the word Email was used as placeholder text in the email text field itself, while in the customer sign-in page, there was no placeholder text there at all.

This is an example of some of the affordances that testing frameworks (like the Capybara gem for Rails) have built in to make our testing lives easier. They go to great lengths to make selecting page elements simple, and automated tests easy to read.

So don't panic if your tests don't look exactly like the ones we write here. It may just be that the framework you're using doesn't have the same affordances as the ones we're using here. It could have different ones.

So if we add some IDs to our page elements, our tests now look like this:

```
before do
    # create a new user
    visit signup_path
    fill_in 'user_name', with: 'New User'
    fill_in 'user_email', with: 'user@example.com'
    fill_in 'user_password', with: 'foobar'
    fill_in 'user_password_confirmation', with: 'foobar'
    click_button 'Create my account'
end
```

Much better. These we could work with. And now our tests will run!

Add ID attributes to your page elements to make your applications easier to test.

Now, if we really wanted to make things easy for ourselves, the simple fix here would be to add IDs to all our page elements and use them in our tests, and then we'd be done.

But just for the sake of adventure, let's take the more bumpy, less travelled road and instead see what it would be like to write selectors for these elements if we couldn't give them any unique IDs.

Let's start by finding the CSS selector we would need to grab our name field.

One quick, easy way to see the underlying HTML for any control on a page is to right-click it and select *Inspect Element*.

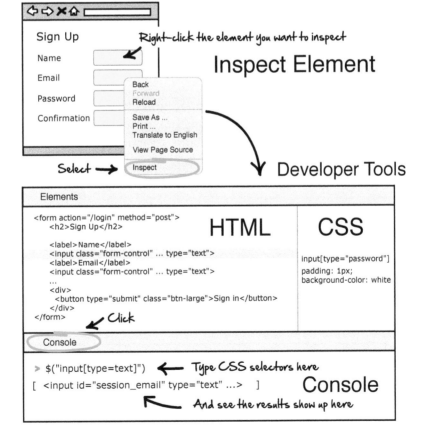

Inspect Element takes us right to the line of HTML code responsible for rendering that control, and it shows us the CSS used to style it.

Another nice feature of most modern browsers is that the developer tools also have a *Developer Console*, where we can try out our CSS selectors.

For example, say we wanted to see if $("input") would give us the text field we want. We could open up the Developer Console in our browser, and enter the CSS.

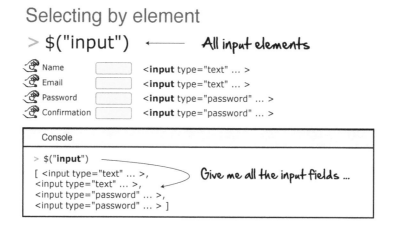

By typing in $("input") into the console window and hitting return, the browser prints out all the page elements matching our selector. In this case, we get all four input fields: name, email, password, and confirmation.

To refine our search a little, we can modify our selector to grab only those text boxes of type text.

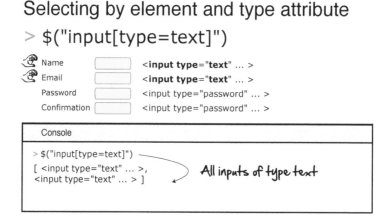

This filters out the password input fields, and leaves us only with two text input fields to differentiate between.

At this point, we don't have any other distinguishing features separating the Name input field from the Email field. So let's grab Name by virtue of its position.

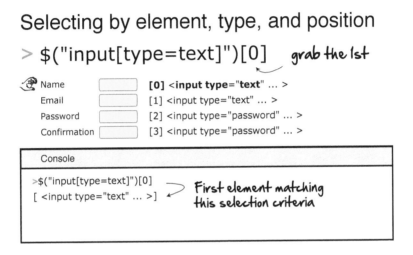

Yay! We got our Name input field. Using that same logic, see if you can now figure out what the CSS selectors would be for the other three.

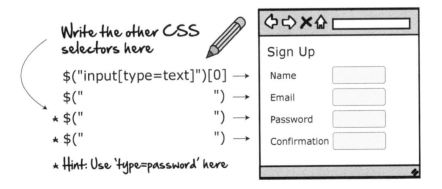

OK. So that takes care of our input text fields. But what about our "Create my account" button? What CSS selector do you think we could use for that?

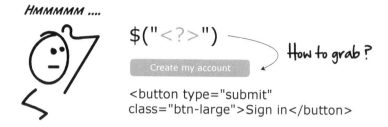

We've got a couple options here. We could select it by its element type $('button'). And if we had more than one button, we could then grab it by its position. But there's another neat way to grab page elements. We can also select them by their *class*.

Selecting by class "."

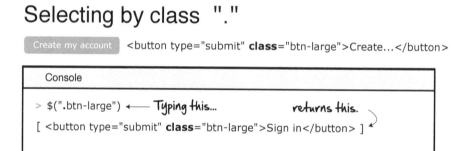

The class attribute is how CSS selectors decorate or apply styles to elements in our web pages. Fortunately for us, we can use this same ability to grab page elements too!

That "." dot in front of the btn-large is the CSS notation for grabbing an element by its class. Grabbing elements by their class is handy when we've got hard-to-reach page elements and we just don't know how to get our hands on them. By decorating, or surrounding, the element we want with a class we can select, we can sometimes get to those hard-to-reach places without having to write a weird, complex CSS selector.

With our button now selected, we have everything we need to grab our page elements.

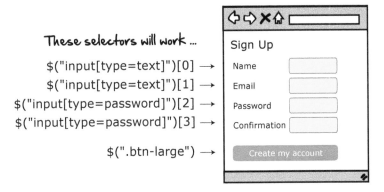

These selectors will work ...

$("input[type=text]")[0] →

$("input[type=text]")[1] →

$("input[type=password]")[2] →

$("input[type=password]")[3] →

$(".btn-large") →

And when we throw these into a test, they look something like this:

```
before do
  # create a new user
  visit signup_path
  all(:css, 'input[type=text]')[0].set('New User')
  all(:css, 'input[type=text]')[1].set('user@example.com')
  all(:css, 'input[type=password]')[0].set('foobar')
  all(:css, 'input[type=password]')[1].set('foobar')
  find(:css, '.btn-large').click
end
```

Hmmm. OK...not the prettiest test code to look at. I don't know about you, but I find this test kind of hard on the eyes. But let's walk through it and see what it does anyways. This line scans the entire page looking for any CSS elements that match our selection criteria 'input[type=text]'.

```
all(:css, 'input[type=text]')[0].set('New User')
```

Then it puts some text into its contents with set('New User'). Same for password.

This line does the same thing, only when it finds the button, it clicks it instead.

```
find(:css, '.btn-large').click
```

It's not impossible to read code like this. It's just a lot of work, which is something we want to avoid when writing tests. It's not immediately clear which elements are being selected, and it's hard to understand what's going on.

This is the downside of writing automated UI tests without element IDs. You get hard-to-understand tests. And worse, this test is brittle. As soon as someone changes the layout of any of these elements, these tests are going to break.

That's why, as mentioned before, the preferred way to do this is to give our page elements unique IDs and write our tests based on these. It's this '#' pound sign, in front of the element ID name, that CSS uses to select elements by their ID.

Selecting by ID "#"

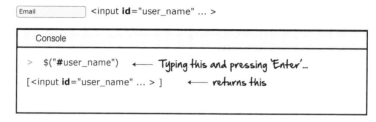

$$\text{\$("\#user\_name")}$$

↖ Select by ID "#"

OK. So that's how we grab page elements using regular, full-on CSS. And if for some reason you can't grab page elements by their IDs, at least you know you can always also try to do it with regular, raw CSS.

With that under our belt, let's forge ahead and make some assertions.

Step 3: Make Your Assertions

Finally. The fun part! Now that we've done the heavy lifting and written all our selectors, here's where we get to sit down and write an honest-to-goodness test.

Assertions are truths we express about our software in the form of code—in our case, automated tests.

Here it would be good if we made two assertions about our login page:

- People with valid credentials can log in.
- People without valid credentials can't log in.

Let's start with the first one.

Testing the Valid Credentials

Judging by this story's acceptance criteria, it looks like there are three things we're going to want to test for here:

- A redirection to a Welcome page
- The user's name displayed on that page
- A success message appearing at the top

Let's start with the first two and leave the success message till last.

If we enter some valid user credentials, hit the "Create my account" button, and then see the user's name somewhere on the Welcome page, we'll know the redirect worked. We can check that with a simple assertion like this:

```
it { should have_content(user.name) }
```

This line scans the entire page looking for the content user.name and lets us know if it doesn't find it.

The success message is a bit more interesting. Here we need to figure out how to select the element containing the Success message, and then assert something about its existence.

Right-clicking it and selecting it with our ever-handy Inspect element tool shows that the alert message is an HTML div or division tag, wrapped within two nested CSS classes.

```
Elements
<div class="...">
  <div class="alert alert-success">Success!</div>
</div>
html   body   div.alert.alert-success
```

What we want to do here is grab this div and then assert that it exists. There are two ways we could grab this alert. We could select it by the first alert class or the more descriptive second alert-success.

```
Console
>   $('.alert')
[ <div class="alert alert-success">Success!</div> ]
>   $('.alert-success')
[ <div class="alert alert-success">Success!</div> ]
```

Both would work here. But because I know we're going to want to check for error messages in the invalid credential section coming up, let's go with the more specific of the two and use the alert-success.

```
it { should have_selector('.alert-success') }
```

QUESTION. WHY AREN'T YOU CHECKING FOR THE PRESENCE OF THE WORD 'SUCCESS!' IN THE MESSAGE ITSELF ?

Ah. Good question. This is a subtle but important point.

UI tests have the tendency to be brittle. The more specific, or coupled, we make our tests in the UI, the more likely they will break. So when writing UI tests, we always try to write them in the least coupled, or least specific, way.

In this case, a tightly coupled assertion that checks the contents of the alert message itself would look like this:

```
it { should have_selector('.alert-success', text: 'Success!') }
```

A loosely coupled, or less specific, test that doesn't check what the alert message says (only that it exists) would look like this:

```
it { should have_selector('.alert-success') }
```

See the difference? In the first case, we're checking for the text. In the second, we're not.

That's the call you'll have to make when writing UI tests: how coupled or tight to make them to the UI. The tighter the coupling, the more fragile the test.

So the trick is to write your UI tests as loosely as you can, but no looser. Loose means not getting too tied to the details. Checking for the presence of things, without worrying about the underlying ever-changing contents, is one way to do that.

But great question. This is probably the biggest pitfall people run into when they first get into UI testing, and it's often one of the things that trips them up.

Keep your UI tests loose. Don't overly connect them to any underlying details.

After doing some cleanup and adding in some unique page IDs, our valid sign-up credential test looks like this:

```
cswp/spec/requests/user_pages_spec.rb
describe 'When creating a new user' do

  subject { page }

  describe 'with valid credentials' do

    before do
      # create a new user
      visit signup_path
      fill_in 'Name', with: 'New User'
      fill_in 'Email', with: 'user@example.com'
      fill_in 'Password', with: 'foobar'
      fill_in 'Confirmation', with: 'foobar'
      click_button 'Create my account'
    end

    describe 'after saving the user' do
      # find the new user we just created
      let(:user) { User.find_by(email: 'user@example.com') }

      # make some assertions
      it { should have_content(user.name) }
      it { should have_selector('.alert-success') }
    end
  end
end
```

The before is new to us here. The contents of this block get run before each and every test in our test suite. We can think of before as a way of giving us a clean slate before running each test, which helps keep our tests isolated and independent. It also sometimes goes by another name: *setup*.

Here it selects and fills out the controls and clicks the "Create my account" button, which then redirects us to the success page.

The describe block assumes a user has already successfully been created, and that we've already been redirected. All we need to do is find our brand-new user and then verify we can see their name and the corresponding success message.

```
describe 'after saving the user' do
  # find the new user we just created
  let(:user) { User.find_by(email: 'user@example.com') }
```

```
  # make some assertions
  it { should have_selector('.alert.alert-success') }
  it { should have_title(user.name) }
end
```

This command is how Rails finds the user we just created, by looking them up by their email address:

```
let(:user) { User.find_by(email: 'user@example.com') }
```

And this is the assertion that lets us check to see that their name was successfully set in the title of the HTML page:

```
it { should have_title(user.name) }
```

Alright. Good stuff. Let's do the same thing now for the failure case.

Testing the Invalid Credentials

The failure case is similar to the valid credentials case, except here instead of getting redirected to a Welcome page, we stay on the same page and get some error messages displayed nicely at the top.

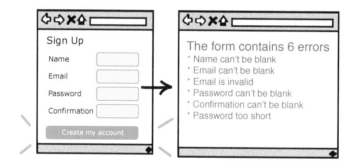

Now, we could write UI tests for each and every one of the error messages. But let's hold off for now (you'll see why when we get to Chapter 6, *Covering Our Bases with Unit Tests*, on page 79). Instead, let's do what we did in the previous section and just verify the presence of the error message itself.

Here's what we see when we Inspect the error message.

```
<div id="error-explanation">
  <div class="alert alert-danger">
    The form contains 6 errors.
  </div>
  <ul>...</ul>
```

And here is the test, along with the CSS selector and a test to check for its presence:

```ruby
describe 'with invalid credentials' do

  before do
    visit signup_path
    click_button 'Create my account'
  end

  it { should have_selector('.alert.alert-danger') }

end
```

Here we are triggering the error message by visiting the sign-up page and then hitting the "Create my account" button without entering any credentials.

```ruby
before do
  visit signup_path
  click_button 'Create my account'
end
```

Then here we check for the presence of the error message with a one-liner like this:

```ruby
it { should have_selector('.alert.alert-danger') }
```

And when we bring together the valid and invalid test cases, the whole test in its entirety looks like this:

cswp/spec/requests/user_pages_spec.rb
```ruby
require 'spec_helper'

describe 'When creating a new user' do

  subject { page }

  describe 'with valid credentials' do

    before do
      # create a new user
      visit signup_path
      fill_in 'user_name', with: 'New User'
      fill_in 'user_email', with: 'user@example.com'
      fill_in 'user_password', with: 'foobar'
      fill_in 'user_password_confirmation', with: 'foobar'
      click_button 'Create my account'
    end

    describe 'after saving the user' do
      # find the new user we just created
      let(:user) { User.find_by(email: 'user@example.com') }

      # make some assertions
      it { should have_title(user.name) }
      it { should have_selector('.alert-success') }
    end
  end
```

```
describe 'with invalid credentials' do

  before do
    visit signup_path
    click_button 'Create my account'
  end

  it { should have_selector('.alert.alert-danger') }

end
end
```

Seeing tests broken down like this may seem a little strange at first, but the way to read RSpec is to combine describe statements like this:

How to read RSpec describe statements

describe "Signup" do
    describe "with invalid credentials" do
        should have_selector("danger")

Signup with invalid credentials should have selector danger.

We start at the top, and then work our way down combining the describes to form sentences. It's a neat way of embedding context into our tests, and organizing them in such a way that we can reuse a common setup. We will talk more about this and other styles for grouping and organizing tests later in Chapter 10, *Organizing Tests:*, on page 163.

What We've Learned So Far

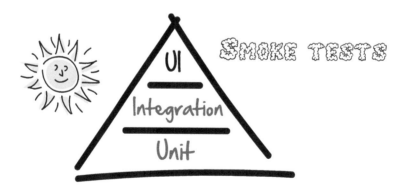

Hurray! We did it. Those were two big chapters on UI testing and we learned a lot:

- What UI tests are and how they work
- What CSS selectors are and how we use them when writing UI tests for the web
- How much easier it is to write UI tests when your page elements have IDs
- How to keep our UI tests loose and avoid test fragility

With UI tests under our belt, we are now ready for the next stage of our journey: integration tests.

So what are you waiting for? Turn the page and unravel some more testing secrets of the web!

CHAPTER 4

Connecting the Dots with Integration Tests

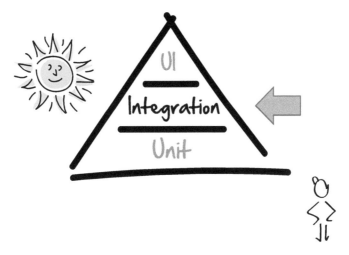

Once you've learned how to write integration tests, the world is your oyster. Not only will you be able to test any back-end web service, you can script and test just about any user interaction you can can think of from a browser, all with a few simple HTTP commands.

Testers, this is a good chapter for you to study so you can start to get familiar with how protocols like HTTP work, which is handy stuff to know if you're going to be testing web applications.

Developers, this chapter will show you the types of things we typically look for when testing web services, and it will give you an alternative tool to UI testing that you can keep in your back pocket.

There Is No UI

Great. Just when we were getting comfortable with UI tests, Dave throws us a curveball. He wants us to test his new back-end permit web service. The only problem is...there is no user interface.

How are we going to do that? If we at least had a web page or something, we could drive tests through that. But without a user interface, we have nothing—only some dangling HTTP endpoints!

What we need here is another kind of test. Something that doesn't need to go through a UI. Something that can speak to the underlying web services, yet is still fast enough to give that quick feedback if something breaks.

Enter the Integration Test

Integration tests are any kind of test that combines more than one thing together. It's a terrible name for a test, because UI tests are integration tests, and technically you could argue unit tests are too (if you consider two objects calling each other "integration").

But in the context of this book, and the way many in our industry use the term today, integration tests for us are going to be the underlying services that power an application. For web applications, these are our web services—programs that run on web servers and respond to HTTP requests.

Integration Tests

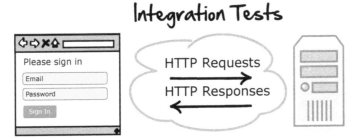

Integration tests are important for a number of reasons. First, they play a critical role in helping us catch low-level bugs we miss at the lower unit-test level.

Good for catching missed integrations

Second, integration tests strike a balance between armor (UI tests) and mobility (unit tests). They give us enough armor (integration) to know certain things are connected, but also enough mobility (speed and feedback) to let us develop iteratively.

And third, they let us test systems at the same level they are built on—specifically, the web. By being able to plug in and write tests at the same level our application services are built on, we can leverage many of the tools and techniques we use when interacting with the web every day, such as our browsers.

If we are going to test the web, we should first get to know the web. Let's quickly review how the web works.

How the Web Works

The first thing to understand about the web is that everything, and I mean everything, is a URL.

$$http://funnycatz.com \leftarrow URL$$

URLs (Uniform Resource Locators) are those links or addresses you see at the top of your browser when you click things in the web. That Facebook update. That banking transaction. That funny cat video. All of those are URLs. And when you click those things in your browser, magical things start to happen.

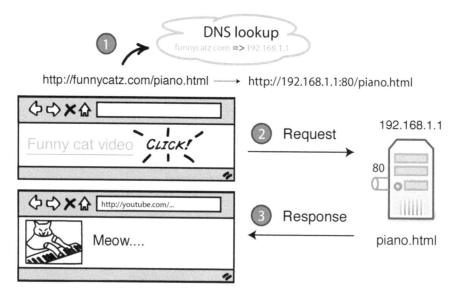

First, a lookup service called DNS (Domain Name System) takes part of that URL you clicked and converts it into something called an IP address. That IP address is the unique address of the server hosting whatever resource it is you're looking for—in our case, a web page called piano.html.

With that IP address in hand, your browser is now able to create the URL necessary to fulfill your request. It does this by creating a URL that looks something like this.

The first part is the *protocol*. It describes the communication standard your browser is going to use when it makes the request to the hosting server. There are other Internet protocols for things like email and file transfers. For us, this is always going to be HTTP.

Next you've got your *IP address*. We already talked about this, but you can think of this as the address of the server hosting the resource we're looking for.

Then you've got your *port number*. Port numbers are the channels that servers are listening for incoming requests on. By default, this is usually port 80, but it could be anything (like 3000 or 8080).

And then you've got the *resource* itself. This is the thing we were looking for—in this case, an HTML web page called piano.html.

With this URL, our browser can now send our request, and hopefully get back a response containing the piano.html file along with all its assets (images and style sheets) required to render this page in our browser.

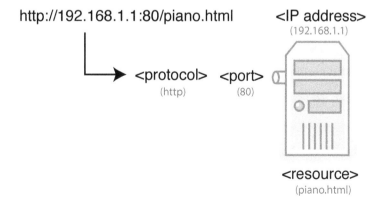

You aren't going to see a ton of IP addresses used in the tests we write (Rails represents URLs for us as variables like login_path). But it's still important that you understand how these things work.

Periodically you'll come across an internal test server that you can only access via its IP address. Now you'll know what that means, and that it is simply the IP address form of a URL.

I'm glad you asked! These URLs—these things we click when we surf the Net—are what we are going to use to drive our HTTP integration tests.

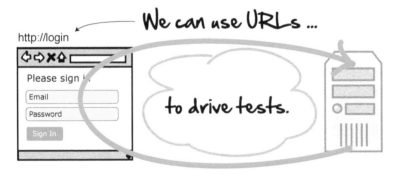

Once we know how to take an interaction in the browser and convert it into its corresponding URL, look out! There's nothing we can't do when it comes to testing our web services directly through our URLs.

But before we can do that, there's one more language we need to speak—and that's HTTP.

Talking HTTP

You might have thought Chinese, Spanish, and English were the most popular languages in the world—but they're not. What makes the world go around these days are three other languages: HTTP, HTML, and CSS (ha!).

HTTP stands for *Hypertext Transfer Protocol*, and it is the protocol the web speaks to send and receive information from one place to another.

You see, every time you click a hyperlink or navigate to another web page, something called an HTTP GET request gets sent from your browser to a server.

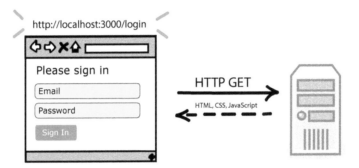

This HTTP GET is a command—more specifically, a verb that says, "I would like to *get* something at this address." In this case, we are getting a web page along with all its underlying assets.

Now, when you fill out an HTML form and click the submit button, another kind of HTTP request gets sent. This one is called an HTTP POST.

There's No Place Like 127.0.0.1

localhost is a shortcut for the IP address of any computer that tries to reference itself locally: namely 127.0.0.1. When testing locally (meaning your integration tests are running locally on your machine), you will often see localhost in the address bar of your browser. All that means is that those requests from your browser are going to be sent locally to this computer.

With that little bit of insight, you can now laugh along at your next cocktail party when someone says, "There's no place like 127.0.0.1." Who said technologists don't have a sense of humor!

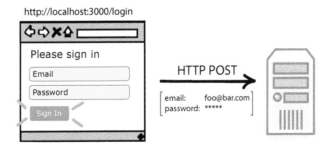

HTTP POSTs are one way browsers send information to servers (see the sidebar for another). HTTP POST takes the contents of your HTML form, bundles it up, and sends it to the server. This is how most login pages work.

Now, the important thing to note here is that every time you click a hyperlink, fill out some form, or hit that share button, your action gets turned into an outgoing HTTP request. Think about that for a minute.

Before the web server can redirect to your favorite cat video, log you into Facebook, or share that selfie of you eating that piece of lemon meringue pie, it first needs to convert that browser interaction into an HTTP request.

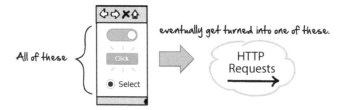

Once you realize this, you'll also realize you have another powerful tool in your testing arsenal—one that doesn't require always having to write end-to-end tests through the UI. But rather, one that slips under the surface one layer deep, allowing you to test the underlying services directly themselves.

This is what integration tests are. Tests that skip the UI, directly test the underlying services, and avoid the pain and suffering that come with UI testing.

Remember our login page UI test from Chapter 2, *Smoking User Interface Tests*, on page 19? The one that filled out the login form and clicked the Sign In button? Here's the same test, rewritten using only HTTP requests and no UI.

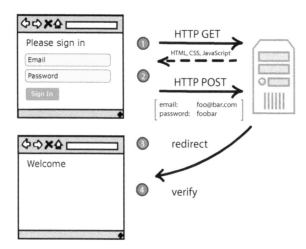

Another Way to Pass Information to a Server

HTTP forms are one way to send information to a server. Another is to pass the data as part of the URL as a name-value pair.

https://www.google.ca/search? q=pixar   HTTP GET →

name-value pair

You do this whenever you do a Google search. Whatever word you type in the Google box gets added to an HTTP GET request and sent to Google's servers. That pairing (a variable along with its value) is what we call a name-value pair or *query string*. And you can pass data to servers by embedding these directly into URLs.

This is fine for simple searches, but it exposes a lot of the internals about your system (which makes it easier for hackers to see how your website works).

There is also a limit to how much information you can send as part of an HTTP GET. So it's not ideal for uploading pictures or lots of data.

That's why you'll see most non-trivial data sent from browsers in HTTP POSTs, and query strings with HTTP GETs reserved for the more simple stuff.

```
def setup
  @user = users(:user1)
end

test "login with valid credentials" do
  get login_path
  post login_path, session: { email: 'user@test.com', password: 'password' }
  follow_redirect!
  assert_select "h1", "Welcome"
end
```

Just like we did before, we start by setting up a fake valid user. We then navigate to our login page via an HTTP GET. We send the login credentials to the server as an HTTP POST. And then we follow the redirect to the new page where we can verify, with an assert, that we have landed at the right place.

If you ever want to see this in action in your browser, you can! Simply open up your browser's Developer Tools (we are using Google Chrome here):

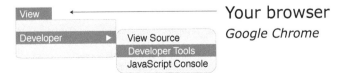

Your browser
Google Chrome

Click the Network tab and reload your page in your browser. You will then see the network traffic between the server and browser that renders your web page.

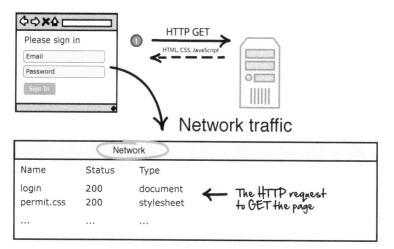

You will see requests of each of the downloaded files needed to render the page. You will see the status of each request (200 means OK, and this is something called a status code; we'll talk more about this in the next chapter). And by clicking any of these rows, you can inspect and analyze each and every request that takes place between your server and your browser. It's handy for debugging and seeing what's going on behind the scenes with the web services you want to test. You can even see the traffic flowing both ways. Just look what happens when you enter some login credentials and hit Sign In.

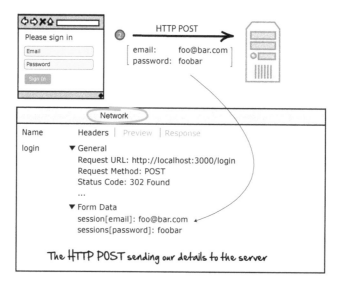

By clicking the Headers sub tab, you can see your actual HTTP POST request being sent to the server. You can see that it was an HTTP POST, what the status code was, and even the username and password itself being sent to the server. These are all handy things to help us write and debug our integration tests when we start scripting HTTP requests from the browser.

We aren't rewriting UI tests as integration tests (even though we could, and that is sometimes a good idea). We are looking at an alternative way to test back-end web services that doesn't require us going through a UI.

Believe it or not, not every web service on the web today has a front end. In fact, many don't. Many are simply web APIs (application programming interfaces—the things people call when they want to talk to our programs) that people create so others can interact with their web services. Twitter, Facebook, Spotify—all these have web services you as a developer can call to get Twitter feeds, Facebook updates, or track information about your favorite artists. HTTP integration tests give us a way of testing those.

Having said that, some teams find testing through the UI so problematic that they do the bulk of their integration testing through their web services, and punt on doing any automated testing through the UI. This is how a lot of Rails applications get tested today.

So view HTTP integration tests as a way to directly test your back-end web services, as well as an alternative way to test web pages if you have a slow, complicated UI.

Alright, with that, we are almost ready to tackle Dave's create permit service. But before we do, there is one other concept that is handy for you to understand before we head out into the wild. And that is a form of web API design that has taken the world by storm. It's something called REST.

What's with All the foobar?

foobar is placeholder text developers sometimes use when they need a value for something, but the value itself doesn't matter.

You may have seen copywriters do the same thing when they insert *lorem ipsum* as placeholder text into documents (which means random text). *foobar* is the developer version of that.

Taking a REST

REST stands for representational state transfer, and it is a simple, standard way to design web APIs.

To see what I mean, imagine you're designing a new photo-sharing site (yay!) and you need to come up with a web API that allows people to create, read, update, and delete their photos on your website. How would you do it?

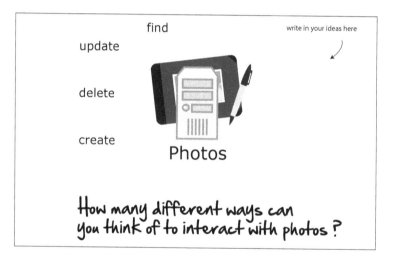

If you think about it, there are literally dozens of ways you could build an API to share photos. You could write a web service called retrievePhoto, where people would pass you the id of their photo and you would send it back to them. Or you could use another similar word such as fetch. That would work too.

Therein lies the problem. Because there was no one right way to describe the fetching or retrieving of resources, everyone created their own. If you wanted to interact with someone else's web service, you had to sit down and learn their customary, proprietary way of doing that.

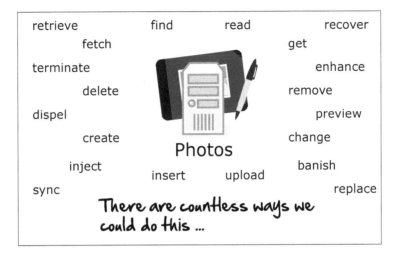

Then one day a smart guy named Roy Fielding came along and said (paraphrasing here):

"Hey everyone. Instead of everyone defining their own way for accessing resources on the web, why don't we just use the name of the resource we're looking for as the URL, and then limit the interactions we can do to that resource to these four HTTP verbs: GET, POST, PUT and DELETE."

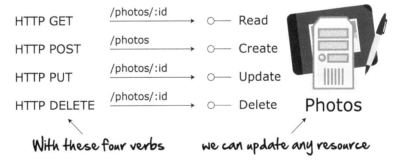

Whoa. This was brilliant. Suddenly, designing web APIs became a heck of a lot easier. Now instead of everyone coming up with their own way of describing how to interact with their resource, there are simply four:

- HTTP GET for getting existing resources
- HTTP POST for creating new ones
- HTTP PUT for updating existing resources
- HTTP DELETE for deleting existing ones

All you have to do is supply a URL based on the name of the resource, along with the ID of the thing you're looking for, and bang! You've got your API.

And that's REST: a simple, elegant, compact way to describe how, with only four verbs, you can interact with any resource on the web. It's gotten so popular that this is how most web services are built and designed today. If this isn't 100% clear, don't worry—we are going to look at a concrete example in the next chapter.

What We've Learned So Far

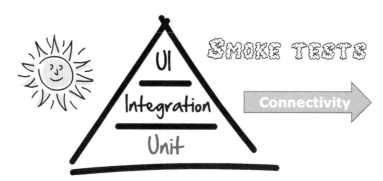

OK. At this point, you've seen what integration tests are, and you know a few things about how they and web services work, in general:

- All interactions in the browser eventually get turned into web requests.

- REST is one style of web service design that lets you modify resources using one of four HTTP verbs.

- The web is made up of a bunch of URLs, which we use to drive our tests.

So that's how things work in theory. You are now ready to put this into practice. In the next chapter, you're going to test a RESTful web service and see what writing integration tests for a web service might look like.

By the end of the next chapter, you'll be in a good place. You'll have seen how the web works, and you'll have some techniques in your back pocket for testing it. So turn the page, and wake up to see some RESTful web services.

CHAPTER 5

Integration Testing RESTful Web Services

No, sorry Dave—we haven't forgotten. RESTful web services have become an extremely popular way of designing web services. If you're a tester, understanding the high-level design of how REST works will help you with the mechanics of your tests. If you're a developer, understanding the underlying constructs of RESTful services is essential for building them. And there is no better way to learn an architecture than to test it.

So with our new insights around how to script web requests with HTTP, and a high-level understanding of how RESTful APIs work, let's now see if we can't come up with some integration tests for Dave and his new RESTful permit service.

Testing the RESTful Permit API

Dave and his team have built a simple RESTful API that enables mobile developers to get, create, update, and delete work permits.

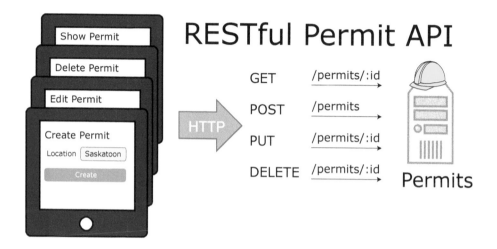

To test this RESTful service, we're going to write a test for each of the four verbs: GET, POST, PUT, and DELETE. Let's start with one of the simplest: HTTP GET.

CRUD: Create, Read, Update, and Delete

CRUD is an acronym that stands for create, read, update, delete—four operations common with any resource we want to interact with through an API.

It's a handy acronym to know, because you will often hear people talk about APIs as CRUD operations. Meaning if they call your API, they are expecting it to support each of these operations.

For RESTful services, CRUD maps to our four HTTP verbs as follows:

- GET (read)
- POST (create)
- PUT (update)
- DELETE (delete)

So if you ever hear someone say CRUD, don't worry—that doesn't mean they are mad. They are just saving time by rolling four common operations all up into one.

HTTP GET

With HTTP GET, what we are doing is *getting* something from the server. In our case, it's a work permit with an id of 1.

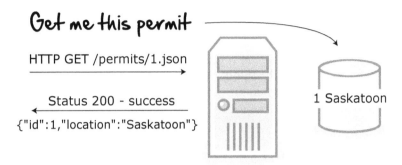

Now look at the full URL used to generate this request.

It's made up of our resource name permits, the ID of the permit we are looking for (1), and that last little bit that specifies the data format—JSON.

JSON (JavaScript Object Notation) is a simple data format we use all the time on the web for sending data. It's an array of name-value pairs, separated by commas, and it makes sending data over the web compact and easy—which is why it's become much more popular than its clunky older cousin XML.

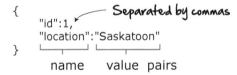

Now, the only thing missing from our GET URL is the GET verb. How do you suppose we specify that? Well, a quick way to generate an HTTP GET, or test the GET request for any RESTful service, is to drop the URL you are requesting into your browser.

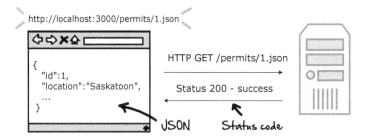

That's right! By simply dropping any URL into your web browser, your browser will automatically send an HTTP GET to whatever URL you are looking for. This is a handy way to quickly test any API. Simply drop the URL into your browser and see what comes back.

Now when a server handles our request, it is going to want to tell us how things went, like whether the request was successful or not. It does this via these things called HTTP status codes.

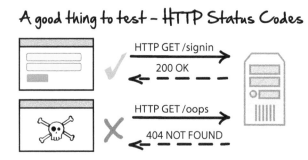

These are good to know because sometimes we want to verify that we're getting redirected, and sometimes we want to check and see what error code we get back if bad things happened.

For example, if we do an HTTP GET and the status code comes back 200, that means everything is fine. If we typed in a bad URL, or asked it for something the server didn't have, then we would get a 404 or "Not found."

Here are some of the common HTTP status codes we often see while testing.

Code	Meaning	Description
200	Success	Everything worked OK.
302	Redirect	You are being redirected to another page.
404	Missing	We couldn't find what you were looking for.
500	Error	Something went wrong on our end.

And when we bring this all together, we can then write an HTTP GET test checking for all these things, which looks something like this:

```
def setup
  @permit = permits(:saskatoon)
end

test 'HTTP GET' do
  get permit_path(:id => @permit.id, :format => :json)
  assert response.body.to_s.include? 'Saskatoon'
  assert_response :success # 200 OK
end
```

This first part, setup, is a useful test construct. setup gives you a place to set up your test objects and data before each test is run.

Because setup gets called before each test case, you can keep the results of one test from interfering with the others. This is called isolation. And we really like it in our tests because this way if one test breaks, it won't break the others.

In our case, we want to create a temporary fake permit that we can use to test our GET method. This setup and corresponding test code create that fake test permit for us.

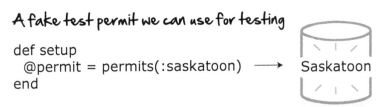

A fake test permit we can use for testing

```
def setup
  @permit = permits(:saskatoon)  ⟶  Saskatoon
end
```

Now that we have some test data loaded, we are ready to query it with an HTTP GET request, which is exactly what this line does here:

```
get permit_path(:id => @permit.id, :format => :json)
```

If this line looks a little strange, don't worry—it did to me too the first time I saw it. Let's break it down and hopefully see it's not as complicated as it looks.

The first word, get, specifies the HTTP verb we want to send out as part of this request. For us, that's an HTTP GET.

The next couple variables are just the id of the permit we are looking for (the one we created in setup) and the format we would like the response to come back to us in (in this case, JSON).

So all this line does is create and send out an HTTP GET for the following URL where localhost and 3000 are Rails defaults:

```
HTTP GET http://localhost:3000/permits/1.json
```

Once this gets sent out, we can then check the response coming back from the server to see if we got the right permit. Fortunately, the HTTP response is available to us in the test.

```
response = {
            "id" : 1,
            "location:" : "Saskatoon"
       }
```

All we have to do is scan it for the word Saskatoon to verify we got the right one.

```
assert response.body.to_s.include? 'Saskatoon'
```

Finally, we can do a quick check for the HTTP status code, just to verify everything is OK, which Rails represents with the :success variable.

```
assert_response :success # 200 OK
```

And that, my friend, is HTTP GET! One down, three to go. Let's keep the momentum going and take a look at HTTP POST.

HTTP POST

The mechanics of HTTP POST are pretty much the same as GET, only this time we need to be sending some data to the server via POST.

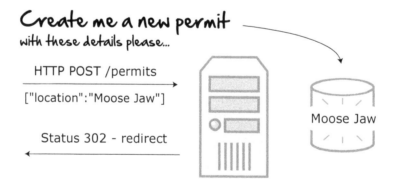

Now how are we going test this? What would be a good integration test that checks to see if we can add new permits in the system?

When faced with writing any new test, one technique that's handy to get the ball rolling is to just pseudocode (write out in plain English) out what you would like to see happen.

Try it now. Use the following space to write out in plain language the steps you would take to create a new permit in the system.

If you are getting caught up in "I don't know what HTTP POST is" or "I've never done this before"—don't worry about it.

Just sit back, relax, and think. What are we trying to do here?

When you do this, ideas will start to flow. Here's one idea. What if we checked that the permit we want to create doesn't yet exist, created it, then verified that it now exists? The pseudocode to do that would look something like this.

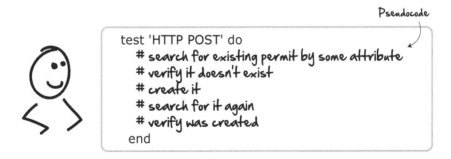

And the corresponding test, along with a status code check, could look like this:

```
test 'HTTP POST' do
  # search for existing permit
  permit = Permit.find_by_location('Moose Jaw')

  # verify it doesn't exist
  assert_nil permit

  # create it
  post permits_path, permit: {location: 'Moose Jaw'}
```

```ruby
  # search for it again
  permit = Permit.find_by_location('Moose Jaw')

  # verify was created
  assert_not_nil permit

  # check status code (302)
  assert_response :redirect
end
```

Here we are looking for a permit that doesn't yet exist (Moose Jaw), creating it, searching for it again, and then verifying that we found it. Not bad!

The 302 redirect is a standard thing many web pages do after you create a new resource. It creates the new resource (permit) for you, and then redirects you to a page saying "Hurray! You created a new permit."

OK. So that's not a bad test. Don't worry about getting your tests perfect when you start. The key is to get going. You can always adjust and try new things later.

Now, just to show you what's possible, here's a more "Rails way" of testing the same HTTP POST:

```ruby
test 'HTTP POST' do
  assert_difference 'Permit.count', 1 do
    post permits_path, permit: {location: 'Moose Jaw'}
  end
  assert_response :redirect
end
```

Now, before I got into Rails, I didn't even know you could do this. This test uses a convenience routine built into Rails that checks the number of permits in the system before sending the HTTP POST request, and then compares that to the number after. If the count goes up by one, we know we've created a new permit. Cool, eh?

Now, either one of these tests will work. One does a slightly deeper check and verifies that the attributes got saved to the database; the other one doesn't.

The thing to understand here is you have options. There is no one way to test this stuff, and the important thing isn't trying to make your tests perfect in the beginning. Just start. Once you start playing with your system and seeing where the various bugs lie, you'll get a better feel for where you need to focus your energy.

Just understand we have options, and we are always discovering new and better ways to test our stuff.

Let's take a look at PUT.

HTTP PUT

HTTP PUT (some frameworks like Rails use a similar verb called PATCH) is similar to POST. Only here, instead of creating a brand-new permit, we are going to update an existing one.

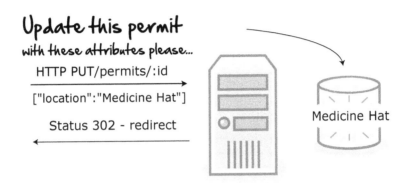

If we go with a similar game plan to testing PUT as we did with POST, we can write a similar-looking test that looks something like this:

```
test 'HTTP PUT' do
  # search for permit by new attribute
  permit = Permit.find_by_location('Medicine Hat')

  # verify it doesn't exist
  assert_nil permit

  # update it
  put permit_path(@permit), permit: {location: 'Medicine Hat'}

  # search for it again
  permit = Permit.find_by_location('Medicine Hat')

  # verify was updated
  assert_not_nil permit

  # check response
  assert_response :redirect
end
```

Same thing as before. We send an HTTP PUT command to http://localhost:3000/permits/:id along with the attributes of our new permit with this line:

```
put permit_path(@permit), permit: {location: 'Medicine Hat'}
```

And then pretty much do the same checks that we did before, only this time looking to see that our permit location changed from Saskatoon, which was set for us via our setup, to Medicine Hat.

OK, only one more. HTTP DELETE.

HTTP DELETE

No surprises here with HTTP DELETE. All we do here is send an HTTP DELETE request along with the ID of the permit we would like to delete.

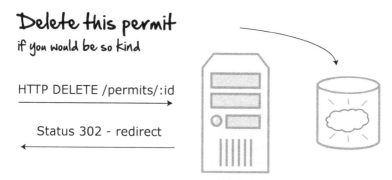

In this case, we can delete the test permit set up for us in setup and then verify it's gone by searching for it after:

```
test 'HTTP DELETE' do
  delete permit_path(@permit)
  assert_response :redirect

  assert_raises(ActiveRecord::RecordNotFound) do
    get permit_path(@permit)
  end
end
```

What We've Learned So Far

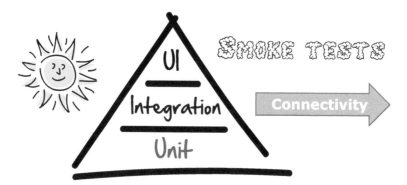

That's it! Congratulations—we have covered an absolute ton here. In combination with the previous chapter, you now have a solid understanding of how the web and RESTful services work, as well as a great foundation to launch suites of integration tests on your applications.

Here's what we covered in this chapter:

- We can test RESTful services by first creating the right URL, and then sending the correct HTTP verb and data.

- HTTP status codes are how servers tell us whether our HTTP requests were successful or not.

- We can always inspect network traffic using our browser developer tools.

- An HTTP GET request is always available to us by simply dropping a URL into our open browser.

In the next chapter on unit testing, we have come to the base of our pyramid, and here we are going to see how and where we do the bulk of our automated testing on projects. But don't take my word for it. Turn the page and discover the awesome power of the unit test.

CHAPTER 6

Covering Our Bases with Unit Tests

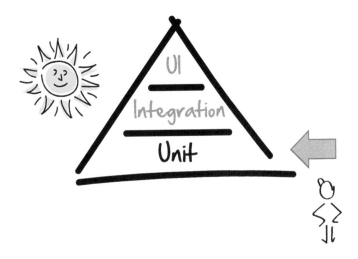

In this chapter, we're going to look at these small little tests developers write called unit tests.

While this chapter is primarily focused on developers, it's a worthwhile read for testers too. Learning what goes on down at the base of the pyramid will not only help testers spot potential gaps at the upper levels, it will also give them great insight into where they should go with their exploratory testing.

Regardless of whether you are a developer or a tester, by the end of this chapter, you will know what unit tests are, how to write them, and why they form the base of our pyramid.

Everything Is Awesome!

Yeah! With our newfound UI testing superpowers, everything is suddenly awesome! Not only can we write high-level smoke tests, but we can also write UI tests for practically anything!

Need a smoke test? UI test.

Got a bug? UI test.

Need someone to fill out that pesky weekly timesheet? No problem—UI test (yes, we actually did that).

Yes, to us the world's problems can now all be solved with one more UI test, and things are going great! Except...

The Challenge with UI Tests

Hey! Have you noticed that our build times have started to take off?

Huh! That's strange. What used to take a couple of seconds and minutes now takes tens of minutes and hours!

And what's up with the state of our builds? Why have they all of a sudden started to break?

BROKEN BUILDS

Beats me! But all I know is with our builds taking longer, and the tests constantly breaking, we are spending way more time fixing broken tests than adding new features to our software.

I thought these automated test thingies were supposed to help!

This real-life story of teams simultaneously discovering the magic and pain of going with lots of automated UI tests is unfortunately all too common.

It's not that UI tests are bad. They are not. They are just not made for the two things we crave above all else when doing rapid iterative development: feedback and speed.

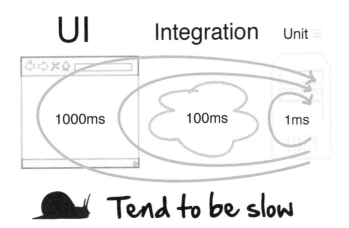

You see, UI tests are slow. Really slow. What takes milliseconds in a unit test can take seconds in a UI test. And while that may not sound like a long time, once you start to get a lot of these longer running tests, the cumulative time can really start to add up.

Not only are UI tests slow, they have a reputation for being flaky and fragile.

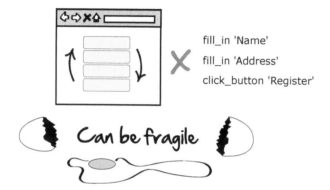

fill_in 'Name'
fill_in 'Address'
click_button 'Register'

Can be fragile

Flaky means they don't always run reliably—sometimes they pass, sometimes they fail (we will talk more about why later). But more than that, because UI tests are so closely tied to the user interface, the smallest change in functionality can end up breaking a UI test, even though it looks like it had nothing to do with it.

Finally, while UI tests are great at telling you that something's wrong, they are lousy at telling you where the problem is.

I KNOW THERE'S A BUG IN HERE SOMEWHERE ...

UI? Integration? Unit?

HEHE

Aren't very precise

Remember—these tests go end-to-end. So finding and fixing a bug can be a lot like searching for a needle in a haystack.

Nope. As good and as cool as UI tests are, they alone are not enough. What we need is another kind of test. Something that's:

- Fast
- Cheap
- Precise
- Gives us rapid feedback

Enter the Unit Test

Unit tests are small, method-level tests developers write to prove to themselves their software works.

For example, say you were writing a program that could play blackjack, and you wanted to verify that all newly shuffled decks contained fifty-two cards. You could write a unit test for that. Something like this:

```
def test_full_deck
  full_deck = Dealer.full_deck
  assert_equal(52, full_deck.count)
end
```

Unlike UI and integration tests, unit tests are small and fast. They don't go end-to-end through all the layers of a system. They tend to be more local. And it's this smallness that makes them fast, focused, and easy to work with. You can write a unit test for just about anything—like testing assumptions.

Great for testing assumptions

Assumptions get us all the time in software. Not anymore. With automated unit tests, hidden assumptions can now be tested and verified, along with business logic.

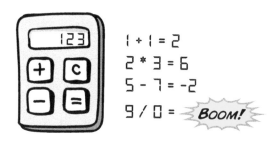

Calculations and business logic

Business logic can be complex. The rules we apply easily as humans all need to be codified and somehow tested in the software. What better way to verify we got the rules right than to code them up in the form of automated tests?

And when it comes to edge cases, unit tests have our backs there too.

$$
\begin{array}{ll}
\text{if (salary} < 100000) & \left[\begin{array}{l} 99{,}999? \\ 100{,}000? \end{array}\right. \\
\quad \text{taxRate} = 30\% \\
\text{else if (salary} < 70000) & \left[\begin{array}{l} 69{,}999? \\ 70{,}000? \end{array}\right. \\
\quad \text{taxRate} = 20\%
\end{array}
$$

Edge cases and boundary conditions

Every time you can think of a new edge case, off-by-one error, or an error in logic, you can write a unit test to confirm these things are working as expected.

For these reasons, unit tests have become an indispensable tool for writing software today. This is why now every modern programming language has them.

Unit tests
FOR ALL YOUR COMPUTING NEEDS

Business logic Edge cases
Program flow Off-by-one errors
Assumptions Permutations

 Instant feedback!

100% Satisfaction! Guaranteed!

OK. So that's what unit tests are. Let's now dig a little bit deeper and see how these things work.

How They Work

At their heart, unit tests are pretty simple. Whenever you add any new functionality to the system, you write a test for it.

Take this new tax-rate lookup feature Dave and his team added to the system. It looks up your tax rate based on the region of the country you live in.

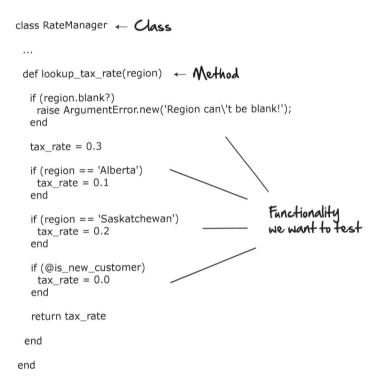

```
class RateManager          ← Class

  ...

  def lookup_tax_rate(region)   ← Method

    if (region.blank?)
      raise ArgumentError.new('Region can\'t be blank!');
    end

    tax_rate = 0.3

    if (region == 'Alberta')
      tax_rate = 0.1
    end

    if (region == 'Saskatchewan')
      tax_rate = 0.2
    end

    if (@is_new_customer)
      tax_rate = 0.0
    end

    return tax_rate

  end

end
```

Functionality we want to test

Now when you look at this code, what sort of test cases come to mind?

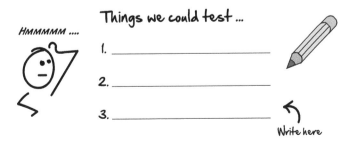

Things we could test ...

HMMMMM ....

1. _____

2. _____

3. _____

Write here

This is what we do when we write unit tests. We look at a particular *class*, see what *methods* it describes, and decide what kinds of tests we'd like to write.

> ## Classes, Methods, and Objects
>
> Three words you'll occasionally hear when developers are talking unit testing are *classes*, *methods*, and *objects*.
>
> *Classes* are the blueprints or templates developers use to create the things that hold a program's data and behavior. You can think of classes as things. A *Player*, a *Deck* of cards, or a *RateManager*. Those are all classes.
>
> *Methods* are the behaviors describing what a class can do. *shootWumpus*, *dealCard*, and *lookUpRate* are all things classes do through their methods. Which is why we usually name methods after verbs.
>
> And when you take a *class* and all its *methods* and you create it, you get what we call an *object*. An object is just an instance of a class. We cover some other good basics of programming later in Chapter 9, *Programming 101*, on page 139.

Now while there are no hard-and-fast rules around what makes a perfect unit test, here are some things we typically look for when writing them.

What to look for when writing unit tests

1. Happy paths	Assuming everything goes right, what does the method do under ideal conditions?
2. Special cases	Are there any special conditions or edge cases that we should pay special attention to?
3. Exceptions	Under what conditions or exceptions might this method possibly break?
4. Program logic and flow	Do all the programming paths, logic flow, and conditional branches work?
5. Anything else!	What else would it take to give us real confidence this method is working?

Happy path is a term we use to describe a test scenario where everything goes right. As developers we are usually pretty good at testing the happy path.

Where we tend to struggle a bit is when things go wrong. That's the stuff we usually skip—which is exactly what we want to start looking at more closely with our unit tests. Exceptions, those nasty off-by-one errors, all that great stuff.

So now if we look at our lookup_tax_rate method again through this lens of exceptions and special cases, a few more things pop out.

```ruby
class RateManager

  attr_accessor :is_new_customer

  def initialize(is_new_customer)
    @is_new_customer = is_new_customer
  end

  def lookup_tax_rate(region)
```
Exceptions 〰

```ruby
    if (region.blank?)
      raise ArgumentError.new('Region can\'t be blank!');
    end
```

```ruby
    tax_rate = 0.3
```
— *Default behavior*

```ruby
    if (region == 'Alberta')
      tax_rate = 0.1
    end
```
— *Special cases*

```ruby
    if (region == 'Saskatchewan')
      tax_rate = 0.2
    end
```

```ruby
    if (@is_new_customer)
      tax_rate = 0.0
    end
```
— *Edge cases*

```ruby
    return tax_rate

  end

end
```
Hint: Look for 'if' statements

First, we could do a little method input validation and ensure that when someone calls our lookup_tax_rate method, we make it known that they have to pass us a region, or else they will get an error.

```ruby
def test_error
  assert_raises(ArgumentError) {@manager.lookup_tax_rate(nil)}
end
```

Here we can do that by passing in nil (Ruby's way of saying nothing) into our RateManager and then verifying we get an error.

Next, we could test one of our happy path scenarios, and just see what the default rate is for any given region. In this case, it's 0.3, just like we'd expect.

```ruby
def test_default_behaviour
  assert_equal(0.3, @manager.lookup_tax_rate('SomeRegion'))
end
```

And after that we could go through any special cases or edge cases we need to handle. Like verifying that those regions with their own tax rates get looked up correctly.

```ruby
def test_special_cases
  assert_equal(0.1, @manager.lookup_tax_rate('Alberta'))
  assert_equal(0.2, @manager.lookup_tax_rate('Saskatchewan'))
end
```

Along with this special deal Dave kindly gives first-time customers.

```ruby
def test_edge_cases
  @manager_new_customer = RateManager.new(true)
  assert_equal(0.0, @manager_new_customer.lookup_tax_rate('Alberta'))
end
```

Awesome! Those are all typical examples of tests we would write when unit testing code.

One last important thing about unit tests (actually all tests): naming.

We want to give our test methods good, intention-revealing names. So renaming these test methods to things that describe what it is we are trying to test is always a good idea. Something like this:

```ruby
cswp/test/models/rate_manager_with_names_test.rb
require 'test_helper'

class RateManagerTest < MiniTest::Test

  def setup
    @manager = RateManager.new(false) # not new customer
  end

  def test_region_required
    assert_raises(ArgumentError) {@manager.lookup_tax_rate(nil)}
  end

  def test_default_tax_rate
    assert_equal(0.3, @manager.lookup_tax_rate('SomeRegion'))
  end

  def test_supported_provinces
    assert_equal(0.1, @manager.lookup_tax_rate('Alberta'))
    assert_equal(0.2, @manager.lookup_tax_rate('Saskatchewan'))
  end

  def test_new_customer
    @manager_new_customer = RateManager.new(true)
    assert_equal(0.0, @manager_new_customer.lookup_tax_rate('Alberta'))
  end

end
```

See the names on these test methods? They do a much better job describing *what* it is we are testing and aren't so focused on the *how*.

Picking good test names takes time and practice. Don't be discouraged if you find picking test names tricky. Just start by describing what it is you are trying to test and iterating from there. We'll talk more about naming later in Chapter 10, *Organizing Tests:*, on page 163.

> **Two Hard Things**
>
> There are two hard things that are a real challenge in computer science:
>
> 1. Caching
>
> 2. Naming things
>
> 3. Off-by-one errors
>
> Ha!

QUESTION!!! HOW DO I KNOW WHEN I'VE WRITTEN ENOUGH TESTS !?

Ah. The million dollar question. This is a tricky one.

Testing is about confidence. You want to feel good about your code—that's why we write tests. One measure of "have we created enough tests" is how confident you feel about your code. And by "feel about your code," I mean pushing it into production. In other words, shipping it!

I realize that's not very useful advice, let's look at a few other things we can do.

1. Make Sure It Works

Does the code do what it needs to do? Sounds obvious. But this is the most important thing you could test. Demonstrating, via a test, what the code does and how it's supposed to work.

Not only will this give you confidence that your code works, it will show others your code's intent. This can be like gold for those coming behind you.

2. Test Everything That Could Possibly Break

"Test everything that could possibly break"[1] is a mantra we use in Extreme Programming[2] to guide ourselves when writing tests. It means if there is a reasonable chance something could break, test it.

Now of course we can't test everything. That would take too long and be too expensive. But common errors, edge cases, special conditions, and anything else that is likely to break are all good candidates. It's definitely a gray area. But the good news is that it becomes less gray the more tests you write.

3. Write Your Tests First

Writing tests first is the practice where you write a failing test first, and then add the production code that makes the test pass after. This is what is sometimes referred to as test-driven development, or TDD. While it may sound backwards, doing this has a number of advantages:

- You build only what you need.
- You design and build your systems in a testable, modular way.
- You end up with a nice suite of unit tests proving that your stuff works.

I don't write the tests first all the time. Sometimes I don't know what I want to test, and I need to sit down and hack things out. When you have a clear sense about what you need, try writing your tests first and see if it gives you code you feel comfortable with, as opposed to writing tests last (or worse, not at all). For a good book on TDD, see Kent Beck's *Test-Driven Development: By Example [Bec02]*. We'll talk more about TDD in Chapter 12, *Writing Tests First*, on page 199.

---

1.   http://c2.com/cgi/wiki?TestEverythingThatCouldPossiblyBreak
2.   http://www.agilenutshell.com/xp

Code coverage is where you run your unit tests against your code, and a tool tracks and sees what percentage of your code your tests cover.

I am usually not a huge fan of tracking code coverage (people tend to get fixated on the coverage and think less about writing good tests). But if you have an old code base, and you are writing tests after, code coverage can be handy for showing you where in your code base you are lacking tests.

Just to be clear though, it's way better to have 30% unit test coverage with some good unit tests, than 100% with some really bad ones. Good teams usually land somewhere in the 70–80% range.

So don't get stressed if your code coverage isn't immediately high. Just keep writing as many little tests as you can and try adding a test every time you add new functionality. Before long, your coverage will naturally start to climb.

Alright. That's one textbook example of how to write unit tests. Let's now look at something a little more advanced.

Turning It Up

In the spirit of innovation, Dave and the team have decided that what their mobile construction app really needs is music.

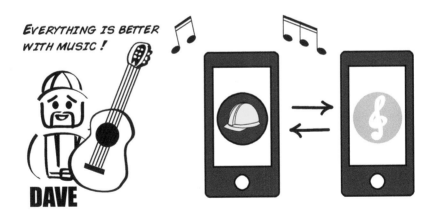

Using an SDK (software development kit) from an up-and-coming music provider, Dave and his team have figured out that if you send a Hello message, followed by an Authenticate message, you can remote control and play music through your app!

The code for sending the messages looks like this.

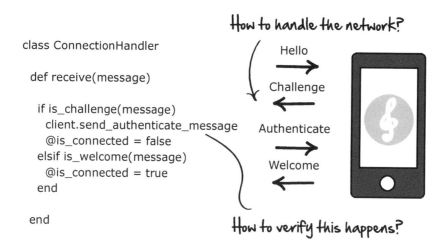

The problem is Dave and company aren't sure how to test it.

For the message handling to work, a live music-streaming service would have to be up and running in order to receive the incoming Hello and Authenticate requests.

But we don't want to do that, because constantly having to run a music-streaming service in the background is a huge pain in the butt. Not to mention flaky and problematic. That'll be challenge number one.

Challenge number two will be trying to figure out how to get our hands on that client object that sends the authenticate message.

```
if is_challenge(message)
     client.send_authenticate_message
```

It would be nice to write a test that verifies that client.send_authenticate_message gets called every time the Challenge message is received.

The only problem is we have no way of knowing when the Challenge message is received because we don't have access to the client object from our unit tests. We'll have to figure out something there.

But let's start with the network.

One way to deal with networks in unit tests is simply pretend they are not there. Instead of calling the network directly, just take the data the network call would have normally returned and use it directly in your test instead.

Pretend you already got the data

```
def test_is_challenge
  message = { :type => 'challenge' }
  assert(@connection_handler.is_challenge(message))
end

def test_is_welcome
  message = { :type => 'welcome' }
  assert(@connection_handler.is_welcome(message))
end
```

Challenge

Welcome

and here you are just passing it in

The advantage of writing unit tests this way is that we are no longer tied to the network. We are decoupled from it (meaning we are no longer dependent on it). This makes our tests easier to write and our software easier to test. We just need to make sure that if the message from the server changes, we will update our test messages accordingly.

Avoid connecting directly to the network when writing unit tests. Use raw test data instead.

Now the next thing to verify is that when a challenge message is received, an authentication message gets sent out. But there's our problem. We have no way of getting our hands on the client object in our unit test.

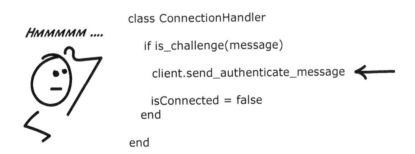

HMMMMM ....

```
class ConnectionHandler

  if is_challenge(message)

    client.send_authenticate_message

    isConnected = false
  end

end
```

This is a classic problem in unit testing. The thing you want to test isn't available to you in your unit test. Sometimes this is a reflection of how we've done our design. But mostly it's because when most people write code these days, they don't write it with testing in mind. It's de-testable (ha!).

One technique for dealing with this conundrum is to inject the class you want to monitor into the constructor of the class you want to test.

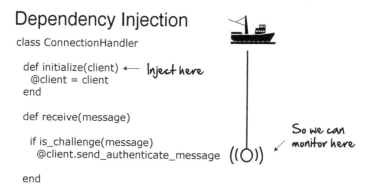

We call this *dependency injection* and it, along with a technique known as *mocking*, is a way we get our hands on objects within test methods we want to test.

Mocks are fake objects we sometimes use in testing to record things that happen to our objects when in a test. For example, in this case we want to know if @client.send_authenticate_message is called when a challenge message is received by our ConnectionHandler.

Our regular @client object—the one we would normally use when running the application—can't tell us if it's been called. It doesn't have the smarts or ability to record when methods are called on it. But mocks do.

So instead of using a real @client object here, we inject a fake one or a mock that can. Then, when we run the test, we can ask the mock if its send_authenticate_message method was called. If it was, we know our code worked.

To make this work in our test, we first need to create a mock for our Client class, and then inject it into our ConnectionHandler via its constructor. To help us create our mock in Rails, we are using a gem called Mocha.

```
class ConnectionHandlerTest < MiniTest::Test

  def setup
    @mockClient = mock()
    @connection_handler = ConnectionHandler.new(@mockClient)
  end
```

Then we need to set some expectations on our client mock. In this case, we expect our @mockClient to have its send_authenticate_message method be called at least once when a message of type challenge is received. We can write that like this:

```
def test_authentication_sent_when_challenge_received
  @mockClient.expects(:send_authenticate_message).at_least_once

  message = { :type => 'challenge' }
  @connection_handler.receive(message)
end
```

Now we are ready to go. For this test to pass, the send_authenticate_message method has to be called at least once.

```
@mockClient.expects(:send_authenticate_message).at_least_once
```

This happens when we send it the challenge message like this:

```
message = { :type => 'challenge' }
@connection_handler.receive(message)
```

Ta-da. It works! We now know our code can handle a challenge message.

If mocking seems a bit strange and you are wondering why we would even want to write a unit test like this in the first place, hold that thought. We are going to get into the pros and cons of mocking later on in Chapter 11, *Effective Mocking*, on page 179.

But regardless of whether you use mocks extensively or not, they are a good technique to have and handy to pull out if you ever need them.

Here is the ConnectionHandler class and its corresponding test class in all its glory.

```
cswp/app/models/connection_handler.rb
class ConnectionHandler

  attr_accessor :is_connected
  attr_accessor :client

  def initialize(client)
    @client = client
  end

  def receive(message)

    if is_challenge(message)
      @client.send_authenticate_message
      @is_connected = false
    elsif is_welcome(message)
      @is_connected = true
    end

  end

  def is_challenge(message)
    message[:type] == 'challenge'
  end

  def is_welcome(message)
    message[:type] == 'welcome'
  end

end
```

cswp/test/models/connection_handler_test.rb
```ruby
require 'test_helper'

class ConnectionHandlerTest < MiniTest::Test

  def setup
    @mockClient = mock()
    @connection_handler = ConnectionHandler.new(@mockClient)
  end

  def test_is_challenge
    message = { :type => 'challenge' }
    assert(@connection_handler.is_challenge(message))
  end

  def test_is_welcome
    message = { :type => 'welcome' }
    assert(@connection_handler.is_welcome(message))
  end

  def test_authentication_sent_when_challenge_received
    @mockClient.expects(:send_authenticate_message).at_least_once

    message = { :type => 'challenge' }
    @connection_handler.receive(message)
  end

end
```

And that's it! Our very own unit tests proving in code that our ConnectionHandler works against a certain suite of incoming messages. If we get any new messages or edge conditions we suddenly need to handle, we can always come back here and add more. It's a handy suite of tests to have.

What We've Learned So Far

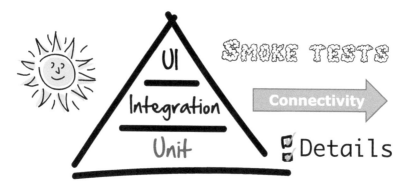

Hey—congratulations. You have now covered all three levels of the pyramid! Here's a quick recap of some of the things we learned about unit tests:

- Unit tests form the base of our pyramid and are where we like to do the bulk of our testing.

- They are extremely quick and great for rapid feedback.

- They are highly local—which means we prefer to avoid things like network calls.

- Mocking is a technique we can use to get at hard-to-reach places in the code that we want to test.

Now that you've got the basics of unit testing covered, it's time to look at a particular kind of unit test that's very popular when testing the logic in our browsers—JavaScript tests.

Let's turn the page now to see what these things are, how they work, and how they can take us to even greater heights when it comes to UI testing.

CHAPTER 7

Unit Testing in the Browser with JavaScript

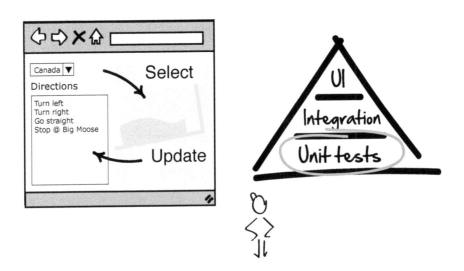

JavaScript plays a big role in the web today, and in this chapter you are going to see why. By learning how to write tests in JavaScript, not only will you gain the ability to test what's going on in your browser, you'll be able to do it in a way that's fast, enabling you to write as many UI tests as you want.

Developers, this will be a good chapter for those of you who write a lot of JavaScript and are looking for ideas around how to test. Testers, you better come along too, as you never know when you may have to get in there and start writing some JavaScript for certain automated testing frameworks out there.

Magic in the Browser

Believe it or not, there was a time when web pages were completely static. No, I'm serious! All you could do was type in a URL, go to that page, and read it. That's it!

JavaScript, along with a technology called Ajax, changed that. By giving users the ability to manipulate and change things directly in the browser, the web suddenly started doing things that were previously reserved for the desktop.

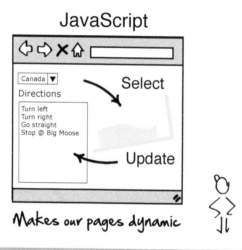

Makes our pages dynamic

The Magic of Ajax

Ajax (asynchronous JavaScript and XML) is the technology that allows JavaScript programs running in the browser to send and receive information to the back end without requiring the entire web page to do a refresh. That may not sound all that impressive, but it was a key technology in enabling some of the dynamic functionality you see in your browser today.

It enabled you to drop pins onto maps. Collaborate with people around the world on documents in real time. And it opened up the web to a host of new applications and possibilities that were never possible before.

JavaScript originally started out as a client-side scripting language. Client-side means the code you program runs in the client. In our case, the browser.

Scripting language means that the code doesn't need to be compiled before it can be run. It can be interpreted and run directly in the browser as soon as it loads. More on this in a bit.

Great question. Ruby is a server-side scripting language. That means that when we run Ruby, we are running it on a server.

Ruby runs on the server

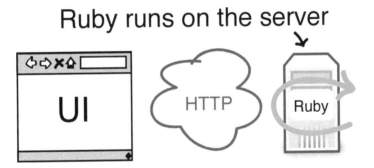

Running on a server means a request comes in, then our Ruby on Rails program does something, and then sends the result back (usually as HTML and JSON). All this happens on the server.

JavaScript, on the other hand, runs in the client.

JavaScript runs in the client

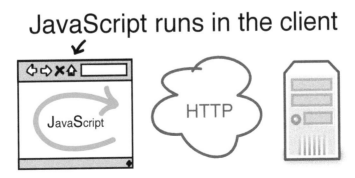

That means all the magic, logic, and calculations happen right in your browser. This is why JavaScript needs to be very fast—it's running on your device.

That's the biggest difference. Ruby runs on the server. And JavaScript runs in the client.

This means we need to write unit tests in both places. All of the unit tests we've written so far have been server-side Ruby. In this chapter, we're going to see how to write unit tests for JavaScript in the client.

But great question. Thank you for asking.

Now technically speaking, JavaScript doesn't just have to run only in the browser. Some people run it in the server too. But for the purposes of this introduction, we will stick to JavaScript in the browser. Starting with something simple like this.

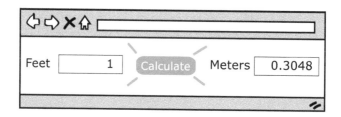

This is a JavaScript program. Actually, it's a JavaScript program embedded within an HTML page.

javascript/JavaScriptInTheBrowser.html
```html
<html>
<head>
  <script language="JavaScript">
    function toMeters(form) {
      var feet = parseFloat(form.Feet.value, 10);
      var meters = feet * 0.3048;
      form.Meters.value = meters;
    }
  </script>
</head>
<body>
<form>
  Feet
  <input name="Feet" value="0" maxlength="15" size=15>
  <input name="Calculate" value=" -> " type=button onClick=toMeters(this.form)>
  Meters
  <input name="Meters" readonly size=15>
</form>
</body>
</html>
```

The JavaScript program is this little bit at the top embedded between those JavaScript language tags.

```
<script language="JavaScript">
  function toMeters(form) {
    var feet = parseFloat(form.Feet.value, 10);
    var meters = feet * 0.3048;
    form.Meters.value = meters;
  }
</script>
```

And the rest is plain old HTML. JavaScript and HTML have a special relationship with one another. HTML is what gets displayed and rendered in your browser. JavaScript is the engine that can manipulate it and make it go.

For example, most of the HTML on this page is for display and layout. But the Calculate button, between the two text boxes, does something different. See if you can figure out what's going on here.

```
<INPUT NAME="Calculate" VALUE=" -> " TYPE=BUTTON onClick=toMeters(this.form)>
```

This line of HTML does more than display an HTML button. When it is clicked, it also calls the JavaScript toMeters method, passing the form as an argument.

```
<INPUT … onClick=toMeters(this.form)>
```

This is one of several ways HTML page elements can connect themselves to JavaScript code. They can listen for specific events and then call JavaScript when these events happen.

Once clicked, the JavaScript toMeters method takes over.

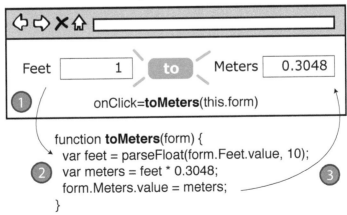

How JavaScript interacts with HTML

First toMeters reads the numeric value for feet from the feet text box.

```
var feet = parseFloat(form.Feet.value, 10);
```

Then it does the conversion calculation.

```
var meters = feet * 0.3048;
```

And then it updates the meter text box after that.

```
form.Meters.value = meters;
```

That's it. Congratulations! You just walked through your first JavaScript program. Every JavaScript program in the world, no matter how complex, goes through the same basic mechanics you and I just did here.

There are obviously more fancy ways to do this stuff, and we'll look at a less trivial example shortly. But that's all JavaScript is. Interacting with HTML. Updating page elements. And reacting to screen events.

Before we look at our next example, let's quickly touch base with the pyramid though. Just to remind ourselves where we are.

Working Through the DOM

While it's not critical that we go deeply into it now, one thing worth mentioning is this thing that sits between your HTML page and your JavaScript—something called the DOM[a] or Document Object Model.

The DOM is a programmable interface that represents each node in your HTML document. For example, when you define a table or a paragraph in your HTML, the DOM represents that programmatically through its API so that if you want to read, manipulate, or update that element, you have the means to do so. The DOM is what your JavaScript calls to make this happen.

While it's OK to think of JavaScript as a way of manipulating HTML, just be aware there is another layer between your JavaScript and the HTML—the DOM.

_____

a.   https://en.wikipedia.org/wiki/Document_Object_Model

JavaScript and the Pyramid

JavaScript testing in the browser can be a bit strange at first because we're combining two worlds we previously kept separate: unit testing and the UI.

Even though we are testing up here...

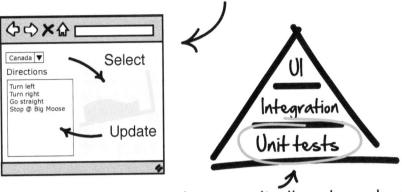

...the tests we are going to write live down here.

The UI tests, as we've defined them thus far, generally go end-to-end. Which is what makes them so great for testing end-to-end functionality.

But UI tests don't always have to go end-to-end. In fact, often it's better, and faster, to run them locally within the UI itself. This is exactly what we are doing here when we write our JavaScript tests.

Now to be clear, these are two different kinds of tests. End-to-end UI tests, sitting at the top of the pyramid, cut through all the layers of our application and go end-to-end.

UI tests can either go end-to-end

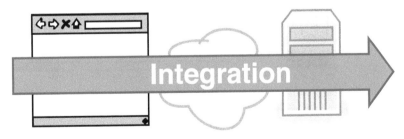

The UI tests we are talking about here, however, will be different. These won't go end-to-end. They will be highly local and test only what's going on in the browser.

Or they can be very local
and test only what's going on in the browser

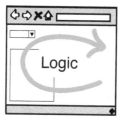

What that means in practice is that you and your team are going to have to decide where your end-to-end UI tests stop and your JavaScript unit tests begin.

It doesn't have to be a hard line. There is going to be some overlap. But what you want to avoid is blatant duplication. That's only going to slow you down.

So just be aware that UI tests don't always have to be end-to-end. They can be local too.

Alright. We are ready. Let's see if we can help Dave by joining him on his bug hunt now.

Bug Hunt

Dave's people-tracker page keeps track of who's on and offsite for any given construction job. And normally it works great. You simply highlight the people on the list you want to categorize, click the appropriate left or right arrow to move them in or out of the appropriate list, and bam! The screen updates itself. No fuss.

Except big fuss! The left arrow button—the one that moves people from the offsite to the onsite list—is no longer working.

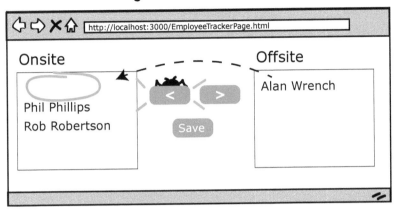

Now when you highlight people on the right, and click the left arrow button, nothing happens. The list doesn't update!

Let's see if we can't help Dave track down this bug. And maybe while we are at it we can write a test to ensure it never comes back too. Let's start with the HTML.

Step 1: Scan the HTML

Whenever you debug JavaScript, it's good to get the lay of the land and see what the HTML that's hosting it looks like.

Here is the HTML code for this page.

javascript/EmployeeTrackerPage.html
```
<html>
<head>
  <meta content="text/html;charset=utf-8" http-equiv="Content-Type">
  <meta content="utf-8" http-equiv="encoding">
  <script src="https://ajax.googleapis.com/ajax/libs/jquery/3.0.0/jquery.min.js">
  </script>

  <!-- include source files here... -->
  <script type="text/javascript" src="src/EmployeeModel.js"></script>
  <script type="text/javascript" src="src/EmployeeController.js"></script>

  <script type="text/javascript">
    $(document).ready(function () {
      new EmployeeController().init();
    });
  </script>

</head>
```

```
<body>
<div>
  <div style="width:auto;float:left; margin-left:20px">
    <table>
      <tr>
        <td>
          Onsite
        </td>
      </tr>
      <tr>
        <td>
          <select id="Onsite" size="4" multiple="multiple" style="width:300px">
            <option value="1">Alan Wrench</option>
            <option value="2">Phil Phillips</option>
            <option value="2">Rob Robertson</option>
          </select>
        </td>
        <td style="text-align:center">
          <input id="leftArrow" type="button" value=" < "/>
          <input id="rightArrow" type="button" value=" > "/>
        </td>
      </tr>
    </table>
  </div>
  <div style="float:left; margin-left:20px;">
    <table>
      <tr>
        <td>
          Offsite
        </td>
      </tr>
      <tr>
        <td>
          <select id="Offsite" size="4" multiple="multiple" style="width:300px">
          </select>
        </td>
      </tr>
    </table>
  </div>

  <div style="clear: both; padding-left: 220px;">
    <input id="save" type="submit" value="Save"/>
  </div>
</div>
</body>

</html>
```

Now don't be alarmed if this looks like a lot of code. It's not. Most of this is just standard HTML table markup. The actual lines of code doing any work in here are relatively few.

Starting at the top, this line here imports a third-party library that Dave and his crew like:

```
<script src="https://ajax.googleapis.com/ajax/libs/jquery/3.0.0/jquery.min.js">
</script>
```

It's called jQuery.[1] It helps them select page elements like the listboxes, among other things, in their JavaScript programs.

Unlike the previous example, there's not a lot of JavaScript in this file. That's because it's all loaded externally from separate files like this:

```
<script type="text/javascript" src="src/EmployeeModel.js"></script>
<script type="text/javascript" src="src/EmployeeController.js"></script>
```

This is the JavaScript code Dave and crew wrote for this page. This is what we are going to test later. Here they are loading it into the HTML page, so they can access and make use of their JavaScript objects like this:

```
<script type="text/javascript">
  $(document).ready(function () {
    new EmployeeController().init();
  });
</script>
```

This is Dave's gateway into his JavaScript code for the page. Here he can instantiate his objects, initialize them, and let them work their magic.

And the rest of the page is just plain old HTML. Fortunately for us, there are only five elements we need to concern ourselves with: the two listboxes and the three buttons.

```
<select id="Onsite" size="4" multiple="multiple" style="width:300px">
  <option value="1">Alan Wrench</option>
  <option value="2">Phil Phillips</option>
  <option value="2">Rob Robertson</option>
</select>

<select id="Offsite" size="4" multiple="multiple" style="width:300px"></select>

<input id="leftArrow" type="button" value=" < "/>
<input id="rightArrow" type="button" value=" > "/>
<input id="save" type="submit" value="Save"/>
```

What's nice about each of these elements is they all have nice unique IDs, which makes them selectable and easy to grab.

---

1. https://jquery.com/

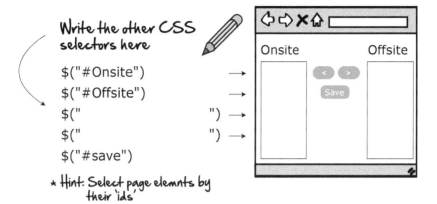

So that's the HTML, and those are the page elements Dave's code is going to be interacting with.

Let's switch gears and take a look at the JavaScript that's going to make all this HTML go.

Step 2: Check the JavaScript

As we saw earlier, there are two JavaScript files Dave's page needs to run: EmployeeModel and EmployeeController. Let's take a look at the model first.

javascript/src/EmployeeModel.js
```javascript
var EmployeeModel = function(){

    function getOnsite(){
        var selectedArray = [];
        $.each($('#Onsite option'),function(key,option) {
            selectedArray[selectedArray.length] = $(option).val();})

        return selectedArray;
    }

    function getOffsite(){
        var selectedArray = [];
        $.each($('#Offsite option'),function(key,option) {
            selectedArray[selectedArray.length] = $(option).val();})

        return selectedArray;
    }

    function getOnsiteIsEmpty(){
        var selectedArray = [];
        $.each($('#Onsite option'),function(key,option) {
            selectedArray[selectedArray.length] = $(option).val();})

        return selectedArray.length === 0;
    }
```

```
function saveParameters(){

    var employees = $("#Onsite > option").map(function() {
        var jsonData = {};
        jsonData[$(this).val()] = $(this).text();
        return jsonData;
    }).get();

    return {"employees": employees};
}

return {
    getOnsite : getOnsite,
    getOffsite : getOffsite,
    getOnsiteIsEmpty : getOnsiteIsEmpty,
    saveParameters: saveParameters
}
};
```

EmployeeModel is responsible for accessing the data Dave's program needs from the page. It reads values from the two listboxes (getOnsite and getOffsite), checks to see if the Onsite listbox is empty (getOnsiteIsEmpty), and saves the onsite parameters into a format that can be sent to a back-end server for saving (saveParameters).

While the EmployeeModel accesses the page data, the EmployeeController controls it.

javascript/src/EmployeeController.js
```
var EmployeeController = function (pModel) {

    var model = pModel || new EmployeeModel();

    function init() {

        var that = this;

        $('#leftArrow').click(function () {
            $('#Offsite option:selected').appendTo('#Onsite');
        });

        $('#rightArrow').click(function () {
            $('#Onsite option:selected').appendTo('#Offsite');
        });

        $('#save').click(function () {

            if (that.model.getOnsiteIsEmpty()) {
                that.showErrorDialog();
            } else {
                that.save();
            }
        });

        return this;
    }
```

```
function save() {

    params = model.saveParameters();

    $.ajax({
        type: "POST",
        traditional: true,
        url: "/tracker",
        data: params,
        dataType: 'json',
        success: function (result) {
            $('#SuccessMessage').html(result.message);
        }
    });
}

function showErrorDialog() {
    alert('Error - Onsite cannot be empty');
}

return {
    init: init,
    save: save,
    showErrorDialog: showErrorDialog,
    model: model
};
};
```

This code here sets up the actions on the button presses. For example, when you click the #leftArrow button, it takes the contents of the #OffSite listbox and appends its contents to #Onsite.

```
$('#leftArrow').click(function () {
    $('#Offsite option:selected').appendTo('#Onsite');
});
```

The #rightArrow click() does the same thing, just going in the opposite direction.

```
$('#rightArrow').click(function () {
    $('#Onsite option:selected').appendTo('#Offsite');
});
```

There's a little more going on with the Save button. When you click Save, it checks to see if the Onsite listbox is empty. If it is, it displays an error dialog. If it isn't, it goes ahead and saves the selected names in the onsite model.

```
$('#save').click(function () {
    if (that.model.getOnsiteIsEmpty()) {
        that.displayErrorDialog();
    } else {
        that.save(that.model);
    }
});
```

Now the reason these objects are called model and controller is Dave and the team are using a popular design pattern here called the *model-view-controller* or MVC.[2]

MVC is an ancient yet powerful software pattern used in many libraries to this day. It encourages you to separate your data (your model) from your view (your HTML page) and coordinate their interactions through something called a controller.

The idea here is that your view should never talk directly to your data and vice versa. All communication between the two should go through the controller. This helps make the code more readable as well as more maintainable by giving your objects clear responsibilities.

Those details aside, let's get to the fun part and see how we can write some tests and hopefully find Dave's bug while we're at it.

Step 3: Write the Tests

We are going to keep it simple when it comes to testing this JavaScript code. We're going to start with the model and verify that it can read those page elements correctly. Then we'll shift gears and test the controller actions, verifying they're doing what we expect them to do.

The testing framework we are going to use here is called Jasmine.[3] It's one of the more popular JavaScript unit testing frameworks, but it is by no means the only one. We are also going to use another third-party library called jasmine-jquery,[4] which helps Jasmine and jQuery play nicely together.

OK, ready? Let's do this, starting with the model.

The Model

JavaScript unit tests are just like any other kind of unit test in that there is usually a setup phase, where you set up your objects and data, and then a test phase, where you run your tests against the data and see if everything works.

For example, to test these four methods:

---

2. https://en.wikipedia.org/wiki/Model%E2%80%93view%E2%80%93controller
3. https://github.com/jasmine/jasmine
4. https://github.com/velesin/jasmine-jquery

Model tests

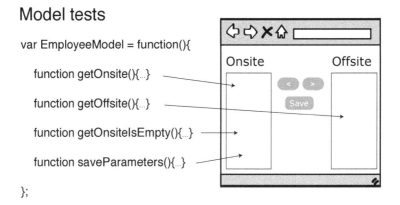

```
var EmployeeModel = function(){

    function getOnsite(){...}

    function getOffsite(){...}

    function getOnsiteIsEmpty(){...}

    function saveParameters(){...}

};
```

We could do the following:

javascript/spec/EmployeeModelSpec.js
```javascript
describe("When selecting elements for employee", function(){

    var model;

    beforeEach(function() {
        setFixtures(
            '<select id="Onsite" size="4" multiple="multiple">' +
            '<option value="1">One</option>' +
            '<option value="2">Two</option>' +
            '</select>' +
            '<select id="Offsite" size="4" multiple="multiple">' +
            '<option value="3">Three</option>' +
            '<option value="4">Four</option>' +
            '</select>'
        );

        model = new EmployeeModel();
    });

    it("should be able to get Onsite", function () {
        expect(model.getOnsite()).toEqual(['1', '2']);
    });

    it("should be able to get Offsite", function () {
        expect(model.getOffsite()).toEqual(['3', '4']);
    });

    it("should be able to get saveParameters", function(){
        var expected = {"employees": [{"1": "One"},{"2": "Two"}]};
        expect(model.saveParameters()).toEqual(expected);
    });

    it("should be able to detect if Onsite is empty", function(){
        expect(model.getOnsiteIsEmpty()).toBeFalsy();
    });

});
```

The first thing we'd do is set up our two listboxes, populate them with some fake data, and then instantiate our EmployeeModel so it's ready for action. That's what this code does here:

```
describe("When selecting elements for employee ", function(){

    var model;

    beforeEach(function() {
        setFixtures(
            '<select id="Onsite" size="4" multiple="multiple">' +
            '<option value="1">One</option>' +
            '<option value="2">Two</option>' +
            '</select>' +
            '<select id="Offsite" size="4" multiple="multiple">' +
            '<option value="3">Three</option>' +
            '<option value="4">Four</option>' +
            '</select>'
        );

        model = new EmployeeModel();
    });
});
```

Once our test page is set up, we're ready to test our model against it to see how it works.

For example, to verify that our getOnsite() method returns the IDs of the employees listed in the #OnSite listbox, we could test that out like this:

```
it("should be able to get Onsite", function () {
    expect(model.getOnsite()).toEqual(['1', '2']);
});
```

This test uses the model to try to access the IDs we defined in our test data, and then asserts that they are equal. The beforeEach wrapper around the setFixtures ensures that the test data is freshly loaded before each test run.

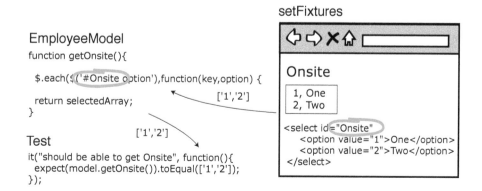

We can do the same thing for the getOffsite(), getOnsiteIsEmpty, and saveParameter methods. We can add some more test data in our setup, give those IDs some different values, and then test the remaining methods in a similar way. This is exactly what we've done.

When we run these tests, they all seem to pass. It doesn't look like we are going to find our bug here.

Let's continue our search in the controller.

The Controller

The controller is responsible for what happens when the buttons are pressed—specifically, the left and right arrows along with the Save button.

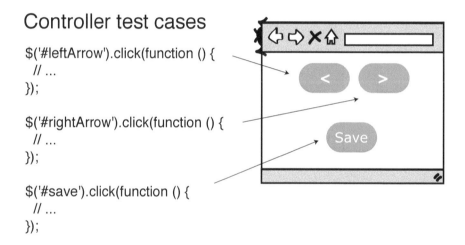

We know we've got a problem with the left arrow, so let's keep the suspense going and save it for last. Let's test the Save button first.

The Save Button

The Save button is interesting because it does a check first to see if the Onsite listbox is empty before doing the save.

```javascript
$('#save').click(function () {
    if (that.model.getOnsiteIsEmpty()) {
        that.showErrorDialog();
    } else {
        that.save();
    }
});
```

Now we don't want to call that.save when we run our unit test. That would do a network call out to some server, and we'd prefer not to call from within our unit test.

But what we could do instead is check to see that the error dialog and save are called under the right conditions. For example, we could do something like this:

```javascript
javascript/spec/EmployeeControllerSpec.js
describe("When saving the tracker list", function() {
    var controller = null;

    describe("and Onsite has people", function() {

        beforeEach(function() {

            setFixtures(
                '<select id="Onsite" size="4" multiple="multiple">' +
                '<option value="1">One</option>' +
                '<option value="2">Two</option>' +
                '</select>' +
                '<input type="submit" id="save" value="Save"/>'
            );

            controller = new EmployeeController().init();
        });

        it("should save", function() {
            spyOn(controller, 'save');
            $('#save').click();
            expect(controller.save).toHaveBeenCalled();
        });

    });

    describe("and Onsite is empty ", function() {

        beforeEach(function() {

            setFixtures(
                '<select id="Onsite" size="4" multiple="multiple">' +
                '</select>' +
                '<input type="submit" id="save" value="Save"/>'
            );

            controller = new EmployeeController().init();
        });

        it("should show error dialog", function() {
            spyOn(controller, 'showErrorDialog');
            $('#save').click();
            expect(controller.showErrorDialog).toHaveBeenCalled();
        });

    });

});
```

There are two tests running here. The first checks to see that save is called if the Onsite listbox has people in it. The second one verifies that it doesn't, and shows an error dialog instead if it's empty.

Both tests do this by making use of something Jasmine calls a *spy*.

```
it("should save", function() {
    spyOn(controller, 'save');
    $('#save').click();
    expect(controller.save).toHaveBeenCalled();
});
```

We touched on mocking briefly in the previous chapter (and we'll really get into it later in Chapter 11, *Effective Mocking*, on page 179), but the way Jasmine does its mocks and stubs is with these little things called spies.

What spyOn does, as you can probably guess by its name, is to spyOn any given object and see if its methods got called during the running of the test.

It's handy for us because we don't want to call the save method on the controller for real. We just want to know that our logic leading up to the call is right, and these spies are a handy way to do that.

OK. After running these tests, no bug seems to be found here. Let's move on to the arrows.

The Arrows

Testing the arrows is similar to what we did with the model. Here we set up our listboxes with some HTML data, and then click the left and right arrows to check that they move people from one list to the next correctly.

```
javascript/spec/EmployeeControllerSpec.js
describe("When adding employees", function(){

    var model;
    var controller;

    beforeEach(function() {
        setFixtures(
            '<select id="Onsite" size="4" multiple="multiple">' +
            '<option value="1">One</option>' +
            '<option value="2">Two</option>' +
            '</select>' +
            '<input id="leftArrow" type="button" value=" < " />' +
            '<input id="rightArrow" type="button" value=" > " />' +
            '<select id="Offste" size="4" multiple="multiple">' +
            '<option value="3">Three</option>' +
            '<option value="4">Four</option>' +
            '</select>'
        );
```

```
        model = new EmployeeModel();
        controller = new EmployeeController().init();
    });

    it("should be able to transfer from Onsite to Offsite", function(){
        expect(model.getOnsite()).toEqual(['1','2']);
        expect(model.getOffsite()).toEqual(['3','4']);
        $("#Onsite").val('2');
        $('#rightArrow').click();
        expect(model.getOnsite()).toEqual(['1']);
        expect(model.getOffsite()).toEqual(['3','4', '2']);
    });

    it("should be able to transfer from Offsite to Onsite", function(){
        expect(model.getOnsite()).toEqual(['1','2']);
        expect(model.getOffsite()).toEqual(['3','4']);
        $("#Offsite").val('3');
        $('#leftArrow').click();
        expect(model.getOnsite()).toEqual(['1','2','3']);
        expect(model.getOffsite()).toEqual(['4']);
    });

});
```

Lines like these two check the values in the lists to make sure our data is set up right for each test:

```
expect(model.getOnsite()).toEqual(['1','2']);
expect(model.getOffsite()).toEqual(['3','4']);
```

And lines like these mimic what the user does when interacting with the page:

```
$("#Onsite").val('2');
$('#rightArrow').click();
```

The first line selects the list item with a value of '2' via our #Onsite CSS selector. And the second one clicks the right arrow by similarly selecting it and then manually firing the button's click() event.

These last two lines check the results. If all goes well, the Onsite listbox should only contain one number, while the Offsite listbox should now contain three.

```
expect(model.getOnsite()).toEqual(['1']);
expect(model.getOffsite()).toEqual(['3','4', '2']);
```

Except it doesn't. The test fails! Which means the bug Dave mentioned is somewhere nearby.

Let's look back over our setFixtures code and see if anything is amiss here.

```
'<select id="Offste" size="4" multiple="multiple">' +
'<option value="3">item 3</option>' +
'<option value="4">item 4</option>' +
'</select>'
```

See anything wrong with the previous code? Anything wrong with the word *Offste*? You bet there is. It's missing an "i". It should be *Offsite*.

That's our bug! A typo in the ID of our #Offsite element. But how could that happen?

This is probably as good a time as any to talk about something that's important to know about JavaScript—type safety.

Static vs. Dynamic Typing

When computer programs run, they apply a collection of rules and checks to ensure our variables and methods are all properly declared and fit for running.

This is called *type checking*, and its main purpose is to help us catch bugs earlier in the code writing process.

For example, if you were to make a mistake in a strongly typed language like Java (say you inadvertently tried to assign a String to an int), the Java compiler would let you know about it.

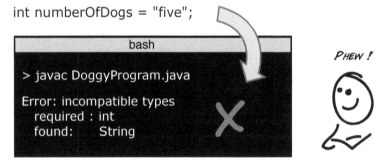

This is called *static type checking*, and strongly typed languages like Java and C# do this check as part of their compilation stage and make you fix mistakes before you can run your program.

What's different about JavaScript is there is no compilation stage. JavaScript is a *dynamically typed* language. Which means no compilation step is required. It simply runs.

This is good in that you can iterate and try out your code more quickly. The downside is if you mistype something, you won't find out about it until you catch it in a unit test or it blows up in your browser.

Dynamic type checking - run time

This is what makes JavaScript tricky. There is no compilation step. That means JavaScript developers have to be a little more careful when it comes to writing code and ensuring that all their object types line up.

It also means unit testing has an even more important role to play. And unit tests, along with tools like jslint (a tool for catching common JavaScript errors), can go a long way toward making your JavaScript more robust and bug-free.

Phew. That was a big chapter. But congratulations! You just walked through your very first JavaScript test. Give yourself a pat on the back.

Let's now open up the floor for questions.

Open Mic

Yes. Good point. When we embed HTML directly into our unit tests, we absolutely run the risk of them getting out of sync with the actual HTML files. If you're not careful, you could end up in the situation where your unit tests pass and your production code fails—precisely because they differ!

That's why many frameworks allow you to load fixtures externally from files like this:

```
describe("When selecting elements for employee - external fixture", function(){

    var model;

    beforeEach(function() {
        loadFixtures('ListboxFixture.html');
        model = new EmployeeModel();
    });
    it("should be able to get Onsite", function(){
        expect(model.getOnsite()).toEqual(['1','2']);
    });
});
```

But there are some advantages to including snippets in your test. For one, it makes the tests easier to read by having the test data closer to the code that's testing it. It's also easier to debug and troubleshoot sometimes when you only look at the HTML needed for that particular test and not the entire page. So it's a trade-off.

Try experimenting with both and see what you like. In some cases you may prefer one over the other.

One of the nice things about working in JavaScript is you will never be short of new ideas, tools, and opinions on how to go about writing and testing JavaScript.

So don't be alarmed if you see many different styles and ways to do this stuff. There is definitely more than one way.

That's why learning the basics is so important. Once you know a little bit about what JavaScript is, how it works, and where its gotchas lie, you'll be in a much better position to judge for yourself which tools and techniques you like.

Don't think this is easy. Some of the smartest engineers in the world struggle with this stuff, so don't feel bad if it feels like it is constantly changing and there seems to be an endless wave of new tools and frameworks coming out. It is constantly changing. And that's part of the game.

Just learn the basics. Keep practicing. And read *JavaScript: The Good Parts* *[Cro08]*. It's a short book (ha!), but it helps with some of JavaScript's more rough edges.

Know that you have options when it comes to UI testing. Not everything has to be an end-to-end test.

In other words, if you are having a hard time automating something end-to-end in the UI, talk to your friendly neighborhood developer and see if there's a way they can cover it with a unit test in the UI.

It may be a heck of a lot easier than going end-to-end, not to mention faster and hopefully easier to maintain.

What We've Learned So Far

Good stuff! That was a big chapter with a lot going on. But you made it.

Key things to remember in this chapter are:

- We can unit test what goes on in the browser.
- UI tests don't always need to go end-to-end.
- JavaScript is not a static typed language—so you gotta watch for typos around the keyboard.

We just scratched the surface of this important topic. If you'd like to learn more, be sure to read other books on JavaScript testing like *Test-Driving JavaScript Applications [Sub16]* by Venkat Subramaniam.

Now that you've seen each level of the pyramid, it's time to bring it all together. In the next chapter, we are going to see how all the tests work in concert with each other, and see how they can all be used when testing a system.

So turn the page to conclude our deep dive into the magic of the testing pyramid.

CHAPTER 8

Climbing the Pyramid

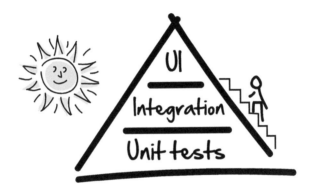

At this point you've seen each kind of test. You know how they work. You've seen them in action. You are now ready to bring it all together.

The goal of this chapter is to just give you a feel for how the pyramid works. We are going to take a small feature, walk each level of the pyramid, and discuss which tests we would typically write where, along with how each kind of test supports and complements the others.

By the end of this chapter you will have a solid understanding of where each kind of test should go, where the lines sometimes blur in our tests, and how to deal with the gotchas that you and your team may encounter along the way.

If there are two chapters in this book everyone on your team should read, it's this one, along with Chapter 1, *The Testing Pyramid*, on page 3.

The Pyramid in Action

To get a sense of how this whole pyramid thing works, let's take our create user feature from Chapter 2, *Smoking User Interface Tests*, on page 19, and see what it would be like to write tests at all three levels of the pyramid for it from scratch.

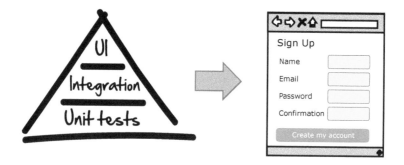

Start with the Unit Tests

Now even though we started out the book looking at UI tests first, that doesn't necessarily mean this is where you should start.

Most teams start with unit tests because unit tests are what developers write every time they add a feature to the system. The idea here is to test everything that could possibly break.

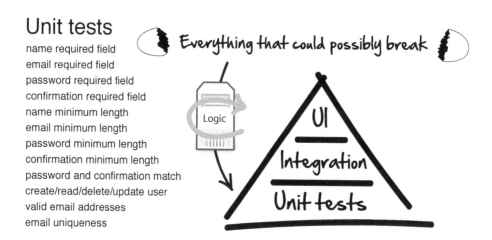

"Test everything that could possibly break" is an old XP (extreme programming) maxim that means, "Test as much of this as you reasonably can, but understand that you won't get it all." We know we can't test everything. But with the right 20%, we sure as heck can test a lot.

Remember that unit tests don't just live on the server. They can live in the browser, or anywhere else you have code too. The idea is to do most of our heavy lifting down here where the tests are cheap, so we don't have to do as much later near the top.

Step Up to the Integration Tests

When we step up to the integration level, our attitude shifts a bit. Here we aren't looking to test everything that could possibly break. Here we are looking for gaps and high-level connectivity.

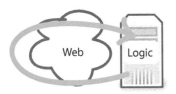

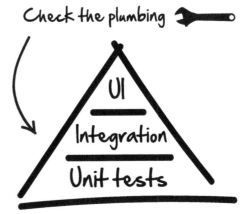

Do the web requests flow down to the database? Is the authentication service correctly connected to the login code? This is what we are looking for here—not the low-level details we already covered with the unit tests.

Now don't be alarmed if you see developers writing unit tests that happen to look a lot like integration tests. This is mainly for historical reasons.

In the early days of automated testing, there was no distinction between unit or integration tests. There were only tests—and developers didn't really differentiate between the two. They would just test whatever they needed, unit or not, and call them all unit tests.

But for us, and for the purposes of our web testing pyramid, integration tests are going to be tests that focus on the testing of our web services. And unit testing will be the testing of the underlying objects.

Good tests for us here would be the testing of our valid and invalid login credentials, along with any of the corresponding HTTP status codes and redirects we'd like to verify are working.

Reach for the UI Tests

By the time we reach this level of the pyramid, we should be feeling good about ourselves. We know we've got a well-tested system. We know we can handle all the details at the unit level. All we are looking for here is end-to-end system confirmation and connectivity with the UI.

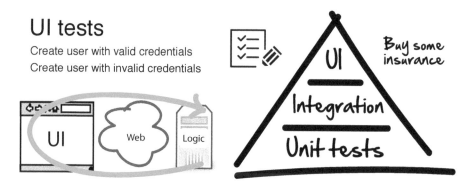

Be careful at this level of the pyramid. UI tests are the best end-to-end tests we've got, and you are going to be tempted to do a lot of testing up here. Don't.

Always push as much testing as you possibly can further down the pyramid where the tests are faster, more reliable, and less flaky. View these tests as high-level end-to-end smoke tests that can be added to projects once the user interface has settled down, and not during early-stage development when a lot of changes are still being made to the UI. That'll just be frustrating.

And don't feel bad if you don't have any UI tests for your system. Not all applications need it. UI tests take the most work to set up and the most effort to maintain, and they are the slowest to run. So tread lightly up here.

Because despite all the pain and cost it takes to set up and maintain UI tests, in certain situations UI tests can be extremely valuable. For example, we couldn't ship our Spotify application to millions of people around the world if we didn't have some form of automated UI testing. We would have to hire an army of testers and spend a big bag of money just to ship our product every two weeks.

I have also worked on super secure, financial trading applications where making a mistake in the UI could cost millions of dollars. UI tests were handy there too.

Don't worry if your pyramid isn't always perfect, or if you think you are writing too many UI tests and not enough unit tests. Half the battle is just being aware.

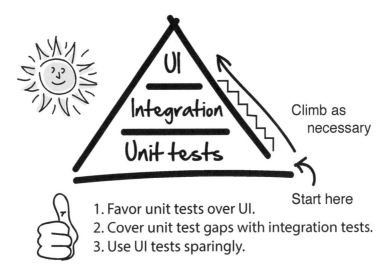

1. Favor unit tests over UI.
2. Cover unit test gaps with integration tests.
3. Use UI tests sparingly.

Now before we go, let's quickly take a look at two common pitfalls teams face when they first start climbing the pyramid: inverted pyramids and flaky tests.

The Inverted Pyramid

The inverted pyramid, or ice cream cone,[1] is what we call a system with lots of UI tests at the top, and little or no unit tests at the bottom.

---

1. http://watirmelon.com/2012/01/31/introducing-the-software-testing-ice-cream-cone

The Inverted Pyramid
aka Ice Cream Cone

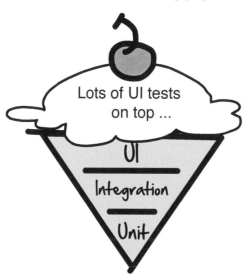

Few if any unit tests on the bottom

Inverted pyramids happen for a variety of reasons. One common scenario is that a team realizes it could benefit from having some kind of automated testing in its application, but no one wants to do it—save the testers. So the team members reach for the one tool at arm's reach—the UI tests—and they go to town automating pretty much everything they can.

The ice cream tastes good at first, but then something funny starts to happen. The testers start to find out just how much time and effort go into making these things stable. Not only that, the tests are constantly breaking with all the changes the developers are continuously making to the app.

The developers want nothing to do with these tests—they see them as a testing problem. And eventually the whole thing either collapses under its own weight, or it trudges along in a zombie-like state and gets chalked up as another failed automated testing effort.

That's one way things could go.

The other way is where the testers and developers get together and collaborate. The developers realize automated testing is as much their responsibility as anyone else's, so they start learning how to write unit tests and start covering the bulk of the test cases down near the bottom of the pyramid.

Push the UI tests further down

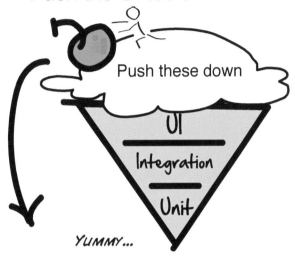

Push these down

UI

Integration

Unit

YUMMY...

to the bottom where they belong

Now an inverted test pyramid isn't the end of the world. Listen to how Julia Oskö, an engineer at Spotify, describes her experience with the testing pyramid.

> I agree with the pyramid in theory, but not always in practice. When dealing with large legacy systems lacking automated tests, then it can be worthwhile to invert the pyramid. Quick wins in terms of low investment compared to backfilling unit tests. Same goes for emerging platforms, like when we started with mobile at Spotify. Originally there was very little support for the different platforms, i.e., no usable libraries for integration/unit testing. So we started with the UI tests, and they served us well at the time.

I agree with Julia wholeheartedly here. An inverted test pyramid is better than no pyramid. And if you can get some quick wins by adding some smoke tests, you should definitely go for it.

Just remember that the inverted pyramid is a place—not our end destination. If we want to continue to make changes to our software, at some point we are going to want to push those slower, more fragile tests that are up near the top, down to the bottom where they are fast and cheap.

So feel free to hang out at the inverted pyramid for while. Just don't plan on staying there forever.

How to Deal with Flaky Tests

Flaky tests are like kryptonite to the automated tester—they sap your strength, slow you down, and generally just waste your time.

What's a flaky test? Any test that doesn't run reliably.

Say, for example, that you have a UI test that logs someone into the system, plays a song, and then logs them back out. When you run that test, it passes 99 times out of 100. That's a flaky test because every once in awhile, when it does periodically fail, you have to stop what you are doing, run the test again, and then hope that it passes. Complete waste of time.

We want our automated tests (all of them) to be highly deterministic. That means consistent. They should run exactly the same way, reliably, every single time.

It's not just the tests themselves that can be flaky. It's everything else that goes with it.

Listen to how Kristian Karl, one of our senior testers, describes some of the things contributing to the flakiness of tests.

> In the book, the expression "flaky tests" is mentioned numerous times. An example is made from Spotify. I have some strong opinions about this. They are (generally speaking) not flaky tests. They are flaky test results. It's a huge difference. It sort of implies where the big problems with automation lie. It's typically not the tests alone. It's everything! The system under test is usually the biggest culprit, not to mention the test environments, etc. The naming of the problem itself can be a problem. Saying it's a flaky test points the finger at the test automation code, when saying "flaky test results" is more of an open question. Which is more helpful for the team, I think.

Flaky tests are also masters of disguise and are great at avoiding detection. They like to lie there in wait and then hit when you least expect it.

So this is what you've got to fight. You've got to resist that urge to ignore them, and instead form a hunting party and track them down head on.

Here are three options for how to do just that.

1. Rewrite the Test

Look at what it is you are trying to test and see if you can test it in a different way. Maybe you don't need to play the song before logging out. Maybe you don't need to book the hotel and the car before canceling the reservation.

Just take a look at the test, see what you are trying to do, and then see if you can do it in some other way.

2. Push the Test Further Down the Pyramid

We should always be doing this anyway, but it's so important, it's worth repeating. Take a look at the test and see if there is another way we can test it further down the pyramid.

Testers, this is particularly important for you. You are going to be living nearer the top of the pyramid, and you are going to see a lot more flakiness up there (flaky tests are more prevalent in integration and UI tests because of all the moving parts).

When you see a flaky test, bring a developer in and show them what you are trying to do. Then see if there is any way you can push it down and tackle it at the unit level. You may not be able to test everything in exactly the way you'd like, but the trade-off may be well worth it because these flaky tests are going to throw you off too. And it may be better just to thoroughly explore it manually and come up with with a simpler, new kind of test after.

3. Kill It—It May Not Be Worth It

That's right. Not all automated tests are worth the effort. If you've absolutely exhausted all options, and this thing is becoming a huge thorn in your side, kill it and cover the risk some other way.

This is what Facebook does. If they detect a flaky test, they delete it—automatically.[2] Why? Because they found it's not worth it. It's not worth the maintenance. It's not worth the disruptions. It's not worth fixing. So they delete it and then just add new tests for the stuff that breaks.

---

2. https://www.quora.com/How-would-you-deal-with-a-large-codebase-that-has-built-up-a-lot-of-flickery-tests-over-the-years

Declaring War on Flaky Tests

Flaky tests became such a problem for us at Spotify that we created a squad (our word for *team*), called Developer Productivity, one of whose main goals was to help other squads track down and eliminate flaky tests.

It wasn't easy (we had a lot of flakiness), but the effort was well worth it. Once we rallied the company around fixing these things, we noticed immediate improvements in our ability to cut releases more steadily and reliably while saving countless hours fixing and re-running phantom broken tests. It just made the machinery run better, and everyone was happier. And while I can't prove it, I think we all lost weight and had better social lives.

You may not have the luxury or resources of forming your own developer productivity team, but take flaky tests seriously, and tackle them as soon as you can. You won't regret it.

What We've Learned So Far

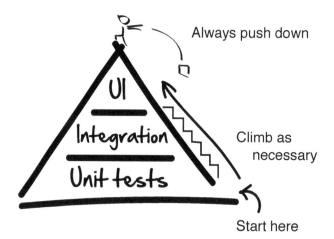

Phew. You made it. You are still here and now you've seen the testing pyramid, experienced some of the challenges we face, and looked at some ways we deal with them.

Automated testing isn't easy. It's a lot of hard work. You never really get there. You are constantly tweaking, learning, and adjusting, but there are a few rules of thumb that can mostly keep you out of trouble. And that's hopefully what you've learned here so far.

If nothing else sticks with you, just remember:

- Do the bulk of your testing at the unit level of the pyramid.

- Catch as many integrations and gaps that you can at the integration level.

- Use UI tests, but use them sparingly. We shouldn't be sweating the details up here.

And that concludes Part I of our book. Congratulations! You are now officially dangerous.

The next step is to turn you into a pro. To do that, it helps to understand a few basic principles about writing code, as well as how to think about organizing all those automated tests you're going to be writing.

But first take a breather. Close your eyes. And just imagine what it would be like to write beautiful automated tests. Then turn the page and get ready to enter the world of programming.

Part II

Exploring the Pyramid

Here we expand on the basics and look at various techniques to make you even more effective at each level of the pyramid. Here you will learn the basics of sound programming, strategies for how to group and organize your tests, as well as some advanced topics around the fine art of unit testing.

CHAPTER 9

Programming 101

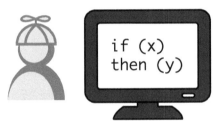

Not everyone getting into automated testing is going to be an expert computer programmer. But the good news is you don't have to be. In this chapter you'll get a crash course on programming and on the thought patterns programmers use daily to write great code.

Testers, you are going to be writing a lot of automated tests in code. This will be a good chapter for you to learn some of the basics around programming structure and to think about code.

Developers, there shouldn't be any surprises in this chapter for you, other than that occasionally reflecting on our craft can be good for helping us explain what it is we do to others. This may be helpful for you when mentoring others.

To be clear, the goal here isn't to turn you into the next Ada Lovelace or Grace Hopper (you'll have to do that on your own). But by the end of this chapter, you will know some of the basics of good programming and how to write tests that are easy to read and a joy to maintain.

> ## The First Programmers
>
> Ada, the Countess of Lovelace, was an English mathematician who is generally regarded as the first computer programmer. While this feat alone is pretty impressive, what's even more impressive was that she introduced many of the concepts we use in computing today back in 1832 when there weren't even any computers around.
>
> Equally impressive are the achievements of Rear Admiral Grace M. Hopper, who was one of the first programmers of one of the first real computers to be created—the Harvard Mark I. Not only was Grace instrumental in programming the Mark I, she co-invented the first compiler for computers, which eventually led to the creation of COBOL.
>
> These remarkable women gave us a lot of what we take for granted today. By learning some of the basics of programming, you should know that you are in good company following in the footsteps of these early pioneers.

The Mechanics of Programming

Not many people know this, but coding is a lot like writing. When we write, we use expressions and phrases to express what we are thinking. We do the same thing in programming, only instead of words and sentences, we use things like variables, methods, and classes.

Take this sentence, for example:

How do you think we could write this sentence in a way a computer could understand? Well, one way you could do it in Java is like this:

int numberOfDogs = 5;

This is called a *variable*. It's an abstraction of some thought or thing we want to represent as data in our software, and we use these things all the time when we program.

For example, to define a variable for a web page we want to test in Ruby, we could do this:

Variables store information

(string) login_page = "http://127.0.0.1:3000/signup"

type   name   value

Variables are made up of three parts. The *type* defines what the variable is. Numbers, like int and float, for example, are types that can be added and subtracted. Strings, on the other hand, can't be added. But they are good at holding words and text.

The *name* is what we humans call the thing we are referring to when programming. Names are important because they remind us what our thing is and what it does. More on names shortly.

And *value*, as you can probably imagine, is the data of the thing we want to store in our variable. For a number, it could be its quantity (for example, 5). For a string, it could be the text (for example, "Hello!").

Not all languages define variables the same way. Java, for example, likes programmers to make the type explicit, and forces you to type it out, along with a semicolon at the end of every line.

Ruby, on the other hand, doesn't require a type—it's implicit, or it figures it out on its own. And Ruby doesn't require any semicolons at the end of the line, in case you were wondering.

Variables are useful because they let us define things once and then use them over and over again in these things called *methods*.

We manipulate variables and do work in methods

```
def setUp
  login_page = "http://127.0.0.1:3000/signup"  ⟵ variable
end

def test_login_page_success
  visit login_page
  ...
end                                    methods

def test_login_page_failure
  visit login_page
  ...
end
```

Methods are where we get stuff done in our programs. Think of a method as an operation. Log someone into the system. Calculate the return on a tax. Display a high score. These are all examples of methods.

When we have a collection of methods and variables that does something interesting, we then collect them together and put them in something called a *class*.

We collect variables and methods in classes

```
class LoginPageTest  ← class

    def setup
      @login_page = "http://127.0.0.1:3000/signup"  ← variable
    end

    def test_login_page_success
      ...
    end
                                          methods

    def test_login_page_failure
      ...
    end
```

A class is a collection of like-minded data and operations. If we were building a calculator, we might put our variables and math operations in something called a Calculator class. Or if we needed a dealer for a card game, we might create a Dealer class and put the cards and shuffle operations in there.

This style of programming—the one we've used throughout the book—is known as object-oriented programming. Object-oriented programming has been around for a long time. It started to pick up steam in the '80s, and today it's pretty much how most modern programming languages work.

I don't want to bore you with the details, but object-oriented programming (or OOP, as we call it in the biz) is exactly this idea of grouping data and operations into these things called classes, which when used get turned into these things called objects. That's why it's called object-oriented programming.

But for now, just start getting used to seeing variables, methods, and classes organized this way, because this is how we've organized our tests. Don't worry if this seems strange at first. Once we get started, you'll see what these things look like in action. It will soon be second nature and you won't even have to think about it.

OK. Next let's talk about the importance of writing style.

The Importance of Style

It was a dark and stormy night. The Wumpus is nearby!

Type 's' to shoot your arrow or 'r' to run away.

```
def process(command)
  if command = "s"
    print "You've killed the Wumpus!"
  else if command = "r"
    print "Sir Robin bravely runs away."
end
```

Just like in writing, style makes a big difference in the clarity of your programming. Style is important because while computers run the programs, it's people like you and me who read and maintain them. So the clearer we can make our code, the easier it's going to be to modify, change, and support (not to mention contain fewer bugs).

To help you with your style, we are going to look at three things programmers constantly do to increase the quality of their code. Specifically, we are going to look at naming, spacing, and removing duplication.

Naming

Names really matter in programming. When we get the name of something right, understanding the program becomes a breeze. Get the name of something wrong, however, and understanding even our own code can be a bit of a nightmare.

Take this little method. You gotta feel sorry for whoever's responsible for maintaining this. It's not at all clear what the author was thinking when they wrote it.

I HAVE NO IDEA!

```
if (val(b))
  redirect :wlcm_pg
else
  redirect :lgn_pg
end
```

Yet when we change a few words and rename a couple variables—bam! The intent suddenly becomes clear.

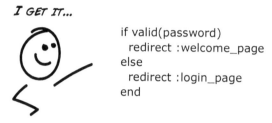

I GET IT...

```
if valid(password)
  redirect :welcome_page
else
  redirect :login_page
end
```

It's hard to give super concrete advice on naming, because so much of what makes a good name is contextual. The perfect word on one project can be confusing and overloaded on another.

But here are some general guidelines to think about when choosing names.

Good names...	Good	Bad
Are easy to understand	salary	s
Make intent clear	brand_color	red
Explain	seconds_per_minute	60
Aren't too long	nasa	nasa_aeronautics_space_administration
Are descriptive	workDays	days
Avoid double negatives	isValid	isNotValid

It comes down to treating code like an author would treat the words and paragraphs in a good short story. You want to be clear with what you are saying, you want the program to be easy to read, and you don't want to make the reader work too hard to see and understand what it is you are doing.

And another element of style that can help with that is spacing.

Spacing

Spacing? That's right. Believe it or not, how you space and indent your code makes a big difference in its readability. Just like reading paragraphs in a book, understanding code gets hard if things aren't spaced and indented properly.

And it's not just for readability that spacing matters. Some authors of languages like Python and early versions of Fortran thought spacing was so important that your program wouldn't even run if you didn't space things correctly!

Naming Conventions: Go with the Flow

Every computer language has a convention for how it likes people to name things. Java, for example, uses a convention called CamelCase, where you alternate the capitalization of the letters when combining words.

```
int highScore = 1000;
String firstName = "Steve";
float myBankAccountAfterComingBackFromVacation = 0.0;
```

Ruby uses CamelCase for defining classes, but when it comes to naming variables and methods, the convention then is to separate them with underscores.

```
int max_number_of_songs_in_playlist = 1000
float currenct_exchange_rate = 2.4;
int average_age_of_hockey_player_in_nhl = 27
```

Whatever language you end up writing your automated tests in, it's probably a good idea if you stick with the coding convention for that language and go with the flow. It will make your tests easier to read and will be less confusing to others following in your footsteps.

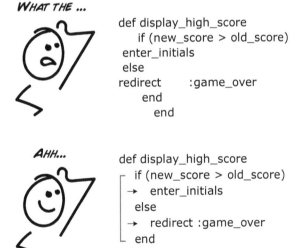

WHAT THE ...

```
def display_high_score
    if (new_score > old_score)
  enter_initials
  else
  redirect        :game_over
      end
        end
```

AHH...

```
def display_high_score
  if (new_score > old_score)
→    enter_initials
  else
→    redirect :game_over
  end
end
```

The other thing that helps with making your programs easier to understand is grouping related things together.

*I KNOW SOMETHING IMPORTANT
IS HAPPENING HERE ...*

```
def some_hard_to_read_test
  get new_password_reset_path
  assert_template 'password_resets/new'
  post password_resets_path, password_reset: { email: "" }
  assert_not flash.empty?
  assert_template 'password_resets/new'
  post password_resets_path, password_reset: { email: @user.email }
  assert_not flash.empty?
  assert_redirected_to root_url
end
```

When you group related things together and add a little something we call *whitespace* (blank lines between paragraphs of code), a big jumble of code can suddenly become a lot clearer. Now when you read the code, you don't have to think as much. You can scan it at a glance and see instantly what's going on.

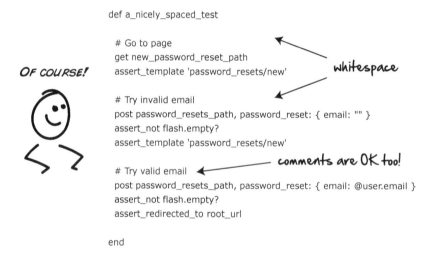

```
def a_nicely_spaced_test

  # Go to page
  get new_password_reset_path
  assert_template 'password_resets/new'          whitespace

  # Try invalid email
  post password_resets_path, password_reset: { email: "" }
  assert_not flash.empty?
  assert_template 'password_resets/new'
                                        comments are OK too!
  # Try valid email
  post password_resets_path, password_reset: { email: @user.email }
  assert_not flash.empty?
  assert_redirected_to root_url

end
```

OF COURSE!

*WHAT ABOUT COMMENTS ?
SOMEONE TOLD ME I SHOULD TRY TO WRITE COMMENT-FREE CODE ?
WHAT DID THEY MEAN BY THAT ?*

Comment-free code is a term developers use to challenge and remind themselves that the code they write should be so clear and easy to understand that no comments are required. It should all just make sense.

While comment-free code is a nice goal and something we should all definitely strive for, there is nothing wrong with dropping the occasional comment in your code to clarify or explain your thinking.

What we want to avoid with comments is redundancy. If the code already clearly explains what's going on, no additional comments should be required. But if there is some wrinkle, a hidden gotcha, or a non-obvious reason for why something might happen in the code, a well-placed comment is perfectly fine and desired.

Next let's look at the root of all evil in software—duplication.

Dealing with Duplication

Copying and pasting code is one of these double-edged swords in software. On the one hand, it's great for quickly getting things up and running. But on the other hand, it makes our code more fragile and harder to change.

To see what I mean, take a look at the following test code. A common pattern in testing is to get the first test working, and then copy and paste the same code for the other test cases afterward, resulting in code that looks like this:

```ruby
test 'can access welcome page' do
  @user = users(:user1)
  get login_path
  post login_path, session: { email: 'user@test.com', password: 'password' }
  follow_redirect!
  assert_select 'h1', 'Welcome'
end

test 'can access company financials' do
  @user = users(:user1)
  get login_path
  post login_path, session: { email: 'user@test.com', password: 'password' }
  follow_redirect!
  get financials_path
  assert_select 'h1', 'Financials'
end

test 'can access plans for world domination' do
  @user = users(:user1)
  get login_path
  post login_path, session: { email: 'user@test.com', password: 'password' }
  follow_redirect!
  get world_domination_path
  assert_select 'h1', 'Step1: Take Saskatchewan'
end
```

The advantage of copying and pasting here is that it is simple and quick. We get immediate feedback with regards to whether our tests are working. That is good.

The downside of stopping here, however, is that if we ever decide to change anything about how these tests work (like logging in with a new password), we now need to do it in three places instead of one.

One way to clean this code up a bit would be to pull all the common code shared between the methods into one setup method, and then call that setup method at the beginning of each test. That code would look something like this:

```ruby
def setup
  @user = users(:user1)
  get login_path
  post login_path, session: { email: 'user@test.com', password: 'password' }
  follow_redirect!
end

test 'can access welcome page' do
  assert_select 'h1', 'Welcome'
end

test 'can access company financials' do
  get financials_path
  assert_select 'h1', 'Financials'
```

```
end

test 'can access plans for world domination' do
  get world_domination_path
  assert_select 'h1', 'Step1: Take Saskatchewan'
end
```

This is much cleaner, much simpler, and much easier to read. The reason you don't see setup being called directly from each method is that setup is a special test method that automated testing frameworks support for doing this sort of thing automatically for us. So in this case, we don't need to call it ourselves.

What we just did here (this small but important act of removing duplication), developers call *refactoring*. In layman's terms, refactoring is nothing more than going back and cleaning your code up. It can include things like renaming variables and picking better method names. But it usually boils down to removing duplication and making the code easier to read.

We want to do these kinds of things when we are writing our tests. Any duplication we see, we are going to want to pull out and get rid of. Doing so will not only make our tests easier to read, it will also make them way easier to change and understand.

> ## Remove Duplication by Continuously Refactoring
>
> Refactoring is the act of improving the design of your code without changing its underlying functionality. That may sound a little weird, but it is an important part of the programming processes.
>
> You see, when we write code and tests, we are in two states of mind. One is to get the test or piece of code working. But the other, often missed step, is to go back and make sure that everything is as clean as possible, and that the code is as simple and easy to read as possible.
>
> That's what refactoring is. It's that critical step that prevents code from decaying over time and collapsing under its own weight, and instead continuously improves it so it remains a joy to work with.
>
> To learn more about this technique and other ways to improve your software, check out Martin Fowler's book on the subject, *Refactoring: Improving the Design of Existing Code [FBBO99]*.

OK. Those are some basic techniques for writing good code. Let's try them out now and see what they look like in action.

Playing the Game

Dave and crew are in a bit of a bind. They've got some code and tests that print a simple little report for each type of meter on their various work permits, but the engineer who did most of the work has moved on and nobody seems to be able to make heads or tails of the code.

Knowing he can count on you, he asks you to take a look at the code and see if there's anything you can do to improve it.

Here's the class and test code for the meter printing feature:

```
class MeterPrinter
  def print(m)
r = StringIO.new
                case m.type
when 'gas'
  r << "Meter Report\n"
  r << "Type: Gas\n"
  r << "Construction Co. Ltd.\n"
  when 'wind'
     r << "Meter Report\n"
     r << "Type: Wind\n"
     r << "Construction Co. Ltd.\n"
   when 'solar'
       r << "Meter Report\n"
       r << "Type: Solar\n"
       r << "Construction Co. Ltd.\n"
    end
return r.string
  end

end
```

And here is the corresponding test:

```
require 'test_helper'

class MeterPrinterTest < MiniTest::Test

  def setup
  end

  def test_print_gas

    header = "Meter Report\n"
    footer = "Construction Co. Ltd.\n"

    gas_meter = Meter.new('gas')
    meter_printer = MeterPrinter.new
    report = meter_printer.print(gas_meter)

    expected = header + "Type: Gas\n" + footer
    assert_equal(expected, report)

  end

  def test_print_wind

    header = "Meter Report\n"
    footer = "Construction Co. Ltd.\n"

    wind_meter = Meter.new('wind')
    meter_printer = MeterPrinter.new
    report = meter_printer.print(wind_meter)

    expected = header + "Type: Wind\n" + footer
    assert_equal(expected, report)

  end

  def test_print_solar

    header = "Meter Report\n"
    footer = "Construction Co. Ltd.\n"

    solar_meter = Meter.new('solar')
    meter_printer = MeterPrinter.new
    report = meter_printer.print(solar_meter)

    expected = header + "Type: Solar\n" + footer
    assert_equal(expected, report)

  end

end
```

Hmmm. While the tests are at least readable, it looks like we've got our work cut out for us in that class. Let's start there.

Step 1: Fix the Spacing

A quick scan of the code reveals that while the test code is spaced reasonably nicely, the class itself is in a bit of a mess. Nothing is lined up. The flow of the method is confusing. And it takes just too much mental work to figure out what is going on.

Let's see what happens though, if we indent things properly and we inject a few well-placed lines of whitespace.

```
class MeterPrinter

  def print(m)

    r = StringIO.new

    case m.type
      when 'gas'
        r << "Meter Report\n"
        r << "Type: Gas\n"
        r << "Construction Co. Ltd.\n"
      when 'wind'
        r << "Meter Report\n"
        r << "Type: Wind\n"
        r << "Construction Co. Ltd.\n"
      when 'solar'
        r << "Meter Report\n"
        r << "Type: Solar\n"
        r << "Construction Co. Ltd.\n"
    end

    return r.string

  end

end
```

Ahh. That's better. We can at least see the flow of the method now and what it's doing. Let's next see if we can't improve on the names of some of those variables.

Step 2: Choose Good Names

Looking at the class code again, one thing that makes this code harder to read is that the variable names are short—like m for meter or r for report.

```
def print(m) # m = meter
r << "Type: Gas\n" # r = report
```

There's nothing wrong with short variable names themselves. But when they hide or make the intent of the code harder to read, that's usually a sign that we want to change them.

Let's go ahead and expand those names and use whole words to better describe what they represent. Tweaking the names a bit, here's what we have now:

```
class MeterPrinter

  def print(meter)

    report = StringIO.new

    case meter.type
      when 'gas'
        report << "Meter Report\n"
        report << "Type: Gas\n"
        report << "Construction Co. Ltd.\n"
      when 'wind'
        report << "Meter Report\n"
        report << "Type: Wind\n"
        report << "Construction Co. Ltd.\n"
      when 'solar'
        report << "Meter Report\n"
        report << "Type: Solar\n"
        report << "Construction Co. Ltd.\n"
    end

    return report.string

  end

end
```

OK, that's better. This is coming along nicely. Now it's clear what this method is doing and what the objects are named. Like Dave said, this method is just taking in a meter, and then based on its type, returning the text representing that meter for a report.

Next let's see if we can clean things up even further by looking for duplication, starting with the class.

Step 3: Tackle Duplication in the Class

Here's the MeterPrinter class. What kind of duplication do you see in there? Grab a pencil and circle anything you suspect you may want to refactor. Bonus points if you can figure out what we should do with it after.

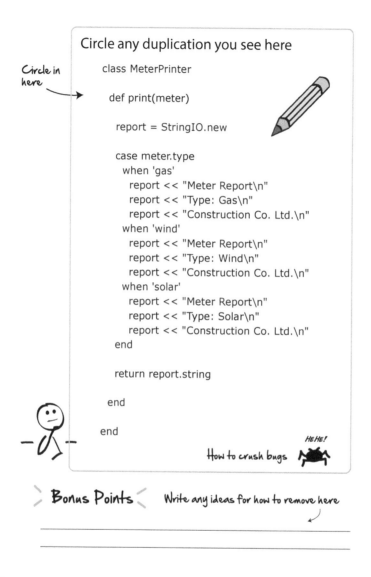

Circle any duplication you see here

Circle in here →

```ruby
class MeterPrinter

  def print(meter)

    report = StringIO.new

    case meter.type
    when 'gas'
      report << "Meter Report\n"
      report << "Type: Gas\n"
      report << "Construction Co. Ltd.\n"
    when 'wind'
      report << "Meter Report\n"
      report << "Type: Wind\n"
      report << "Construction Co. Ltd.\n"
    when 'solar'
      report << "Meter Report\n"
      report << "Type: Solar\n"
      report << "Construction Co. Ltd.\n"
    end

    return report.string

  end

end
```

How to crush bugs HE HE!

> **Bonus Points** ‹ Write any ideas for how to remove here

_____

_____

Hopefully after scanning this, you were able to identify a few of the following culprits.

It seems like the Meter Report header and the Construction Co. Ltd. footer are added regardless of which type of meter is present (a clear case of copy and paste). The question now is what to do about it.

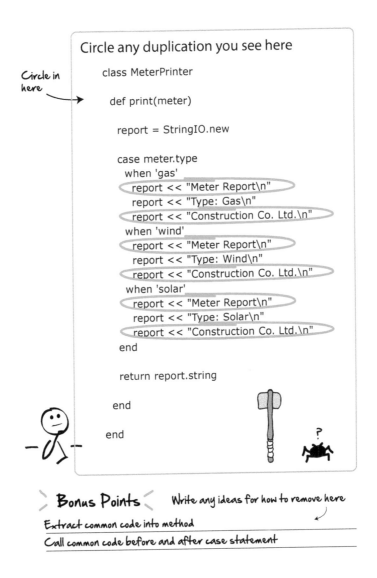

Circle in here

Circle any duplication you see here

```
class MeterPrinter

  def print(meter)

    report = StringIO.new

    case meter.type
      when 'gas'
        report << "Meter Report\n"
        report << "Type: Gas\n"
        report << "Construction Co. Ltd.\n"
      when 'wind'
        report << "Meter Report\n"
        report << "Type: Wind\n"
        report << "Construction Co. Ltd.\n"
      when 'solar'
        report << "Meter Report\n"
        report << "Type: Solar\n"
        report << "Construction Co. Ltd.\n"
    end

    return report.string

  end

end
```

Bonus Points   Write any ideas for how to remove here

Extract common code into method

Call common code before and after case statement

If your first instinct was to pull this code into a common method somewhere, your instincts are good. This is something we would normally do when faced with duplication in a method. Just pull it out and call it from wherever it is used.

In this case, however, it's not only the code that is duplicated, it's the pattern in which it is called. What might make more sense in this case is to simply pull the Meter Report line before the case statement is called, and push the Construction Co. Ltd. part till after. Something like this:

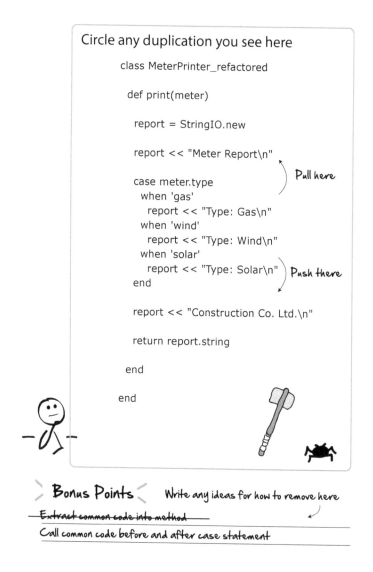

Circle any duplication you see here

```
class MeterPrinter_refactored

  def print(meter)

    report = StringIO.new

    report << "Meter Report\n"

    case meter.type
      when 'gas'
        report << "Type: Gas\n"
      when 'wind'
        report << "Type: Wind\n"
      when 'solar'
        report << "Type: Solar\n"
    end

    report << "Construction Co. Ltd.\n"

    return report.string

  end

end
```

Pull here

Push there

> Bonus Points < Write any ideas for how to remove here
> ~~Extract common code into method~~
> Call common code before and after case statement

Now there is no header or footer duplication in the method, and the code is a little easier to read and understand.

But believe it or not, there is still some duplication left in this method! Cleaning code and removing duplication is like that. After you remove the first layer of duplication, another layer usually becomes clear.

See if you can clean up this code and remove even a little bit more. The solution will be waiting for you at the end of the chapter.

Now let's take a look and do the same thing for the test class.

Step 4: Remove Duplication in the Test

Scanning the tests, we can see instantly that this is another classic case of copy and paste. No need to pass judgement here. We don't know the kind of pressure the author was under when they wrote this. At least we have tests!

Going through a similar exercise with the tests, let's start by circling all the places we see duplication, and then thinking of some options for dealing with it after.

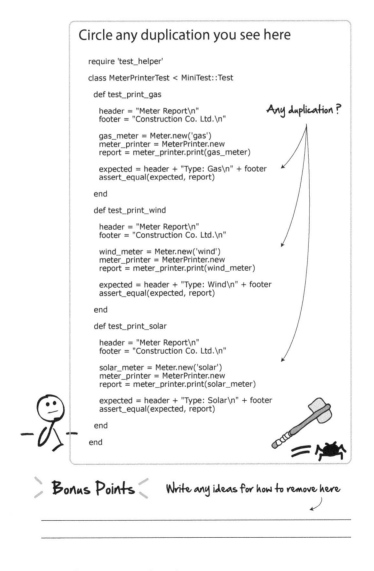

Here's some stuff that immediately jumps out.

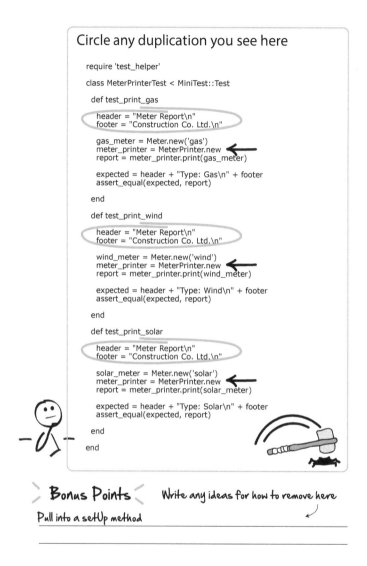

The header and footer variables are redeclared in each test—no need for that. And the meter_printer variable is also redefined three times.

The simplest thing to do in this case is the same thing we did before. Pull these variables up into the testing framework's setup method and then let setup re-initialize them from scratch before each test run.

Remember, setup is a special testing framework construct where we can embed reusable code. That's why we don't have to call the method explicitly in each test—the testing framework does that automatically for us.

Doing that, our test code now looks like this.

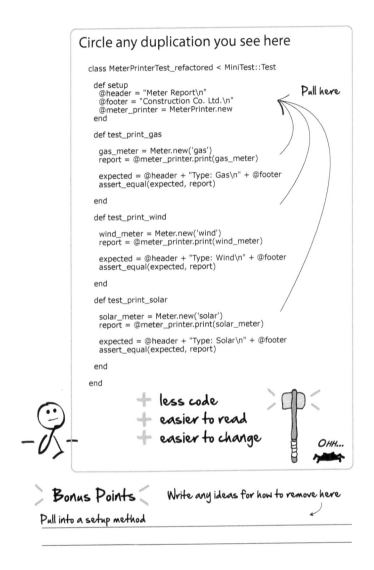

Hurray! Good job. Much better. This is code we could be proud of, and this is code that will be much easier to read and maintain into the future. Future readers of this code will thank you for your efforts.

Spacing, naming, and removing duplication. That's the game we constantly play when writing code. And the fun part is it never ends. You are always going to come up with better ways to express things. So don't worry about getting it perfect the first time—it never is.

Just keep improving the code incrementally as you go, and over time it will get better. Before long others will find your code a pleasure to maintain and a joy to read.

Oh, and here is the cleaned up code courtesy of reviewer Matteo Vaccari, who correctly pointed out that there was indeed more duplication to be removed from the code. Our class is now looking much better.

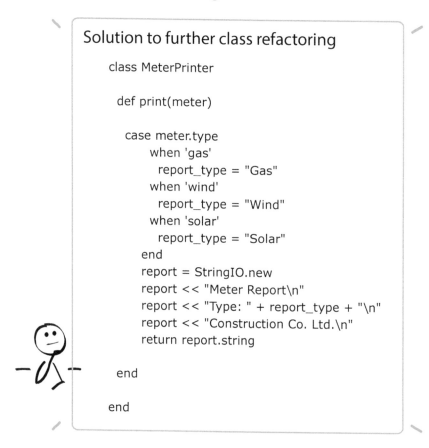

Solution to further class refactoring

```
class MeterPrinter

  def print(meter)

    case meter.type
      when 'gas'
        report_type = "Gas"
      when 'wind'
        report_type = "Wind"
      when 'solar'
        report_type = "Solar"
    end
    report = StringIO.new
    report << "Meter Report\n"
    report << "Type: " + report_type + "\n"
    report << "Construction Co. Ltd.\n"
    return report.string

  end

end
```

What We've Learned So Far

Good stuff! You now have in your possession three handy tools for writing good code and creating maintainable tests:

- Spacing
- Naming
- Removing duplication

All good elements of programming style, sharing the same goals we go after when writing: clarity, intent, and purpose.

There's a lot more to be said about programming, and if you are a tester and new to programming, I encourage you to write lots of tests, read books, and befriend your neighborhood developers. Most will be happy to share with you what they know, along with many other good practices and techniques that they use for writing good code.

With this knowledge under our belt, we are now ready to focus on another area critical to good automated test maintenance: organization.

CHAPTER 10

Organizing Tests:
Bringing Method to the Madness

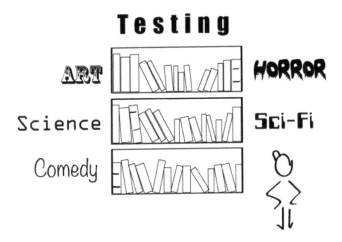

Organizing tests may not sound all that sexy, but the ease and grace with which you can find, add, and update new tests plays a big role in the quality of your test life.

In this chapter, targeted at both testers and developers, we are going to look at two techniques for keeping your tests simple and organized. By learning the art of isolation as well as grouping tests by context, you'll be able to quickly find old tests, easily add new ones, and never be at a loss for where your next test should go.

The Land of Confusion

When the juices are flowing and you are on a roll, it will seem natural and convenient to just want to add new tests to existing test cases.

Take this area calculator test, for example. It calculates the various areas of geometric shapes.

```ruby
class AreaTest < MiniTest::Test

  def setup
    @length = 3.0
    @width = 4.0
    @base = 5.0
    @height = 2.0
    @abase = 6.0
    @bbase = 7.0
  end

  def test_areas
    assert_equal(12, Rectangle.area(@length, @width))
    assert_equal(5, Triangle.area(@base, @height))
    assert_equal(13, Trapezoid.area(@abase, @bbase, @height))
  end

end
```

OK ...

This test is great! It's small. It's short. It's easy to read. Seems like a natural place to add more things to do with geometric shapes.

But watch what happens when we add the ability to test something that seems related but really isn't. Namely, the ability to calculate a shape's perimeter.

Boom! Confusion land. Now we have to rename the test of our class to something long and awkward like AreaAndPerimeterTest. Then it's not immediately clear which tests go with which data. And thirdly, what used to be simple and easy is now cumbersome and hard. We have to think too hard just to try and understand what's going on.

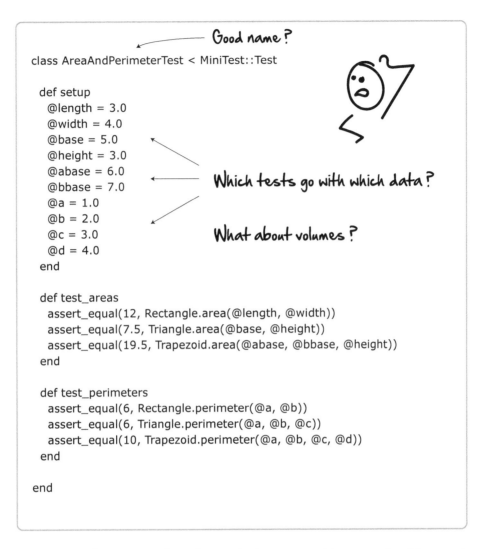

```ruby
class AreaAndPerimeterTest < MiniTest::Test

  def setup
    @length = 3.0
    @width = 4.0
    @base = 5.0
    @height = 3.0
    @abase = 6.0
    @bbase = 7.0
    @a = 1.0
    @b = 2.0
    @c = 3.0
    @d = 4.0
  end

  def test_areas
    assert_equal(12, Rectangle.area(@length, @width))
    assert_equal(7.5, Triangle.area(@base, @height))
    assert_equal(19.5, Trapezoid.area(@abase, @bbase, @height))
  end

  def test_perimeters
    assert_equal(6, Rectangle.perimeter(@a, @b))
    assert_equal(6, Triangle.perimeter(@a, @b, @c))
    assert_equal(10, Trapezoid.perimeter(@a, @b, @c, @d))
  end

end
```

Good name?

Which tests go with which data?

What about volumes?

What we need are some thoughts and ideas around how we should organize our tests. Something that lets us:

- Add new tests easily
- Keep the ones we have simple and easy to understand
- Not make our heads hurt every time we come back and look at it

The Beauty of Isolation

Testing in isolation means when you write a test, try to focus on testing one thing or concept at a time.

For example, look what happens if we rearrange our shape calculator tests slightly so that instead of trying to test all geometric shapes at once, we test only rectangles.

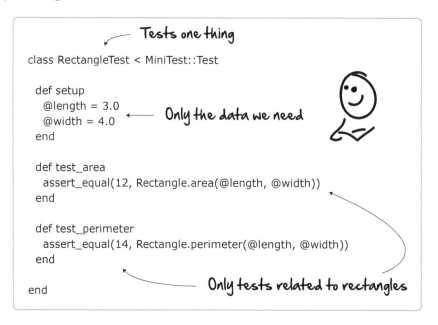

Way cleaner. By focusing only on the rectangle, the test name is now clearer. No more confusing data to have to sift through (we keep only what we need). And all the tests that appear are related to rectangles, and nothing else.

While all our tests obviously won't be this simple or neat, this is the attitude we shoot for going into any new test—simple, clear, and to the point.

We want to be able to come back to our tests repeatedly, understand them at a glance, and then quickly make our changes so we can move on.

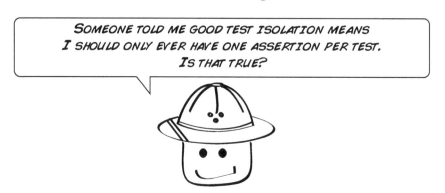

Good question. It's true that tests that only have one assertion per test can be easier to read, maintain, and understand. But it's not a hard-and-fast rule.

For example, take a style of automated testing my good friend Dan North pioneered, known as BDD,[1] or behavior-driven development. In BDD you first describe the context or scenario that you are testing, and then you typically have one assertion per test thereafter.

```
class WhenSomethingHappens

  def setup
    # prepare data/context and do something
  end

  def then_foo
    # assert foo outcome
  end

  def then_bar
    # assert bar outcome
  end

end
```

For example, if you wanted to test the creation of a new card, you could do it BDD style like this:

```
class WhenCreatingANewCard < MiniTest::Test

  def setup
    @card = Card.new(2, 'Hearts')
  end

  def test_that_card_value_is
    assert_equal(2, @card.value)
  end

  def test_that_card_suit_is
    assert_equal('Hearts', @card.suit)
  end

end
```

This is a nice way to write tests (for reasons we are going to talk more about in the next section). You've got a test with clear focus. A nice short name. And writing tests in this style tends to result in many more little focussed tests.

But we could have just as easily written the same test using multiple assertions, and this would have been fine too.

---

1.   https://en.wikipedia.org/wiki/Behavior-driven_development

```ruby
class CardTest < MiniTest::Test

  def setup
    @card = Card.new(2, 'Hearts')
  end

  def test_new_card
    assert_equal(2, @card.value)
    assert_equal('Hearts', @card.suit)
  end

end
```

One assertion per test is a fine thing to shoot for, but we don't need to be dogmatic about it. If you need multiple assertions in your tests, go ahead and use them.

What's more important is the concept of testing one thing per test. If you do that, you won't have a lot of assertions in every test anyways, and your code will be easier to read and cleaner for it.

Test Frameworks Encourage Isolation by Design

Ever notice how you can't string a series of tests together in any good automated testing frameworks? That's by design.

The first test framework designers, like Kent Beck who created JUnit, knew the pain that came with having different tests interact with each other. So he designed the first massively popular unit testing framework, JUnit, so that each test would pass or fail completely independently of the other. In other words, each test was isolated.

The other thing he did was create the concept of setUp and tearDown for tests. Which is where you put common stuff you want to setUp and tearDown before and after the running of each test.

These are just a few of the ways your test framework can help you write isolated tests. Use them to keep your tests separated.

OK. Let's try this out. Here is the formula for calculating the volume of a rectangle. Note there is one new bit of information required for this calculation—h or height.

$$V = l * w * h$$

We are going to add the volume calculation to our Rectangle test. The question is, where do you think we should stick the height variable?

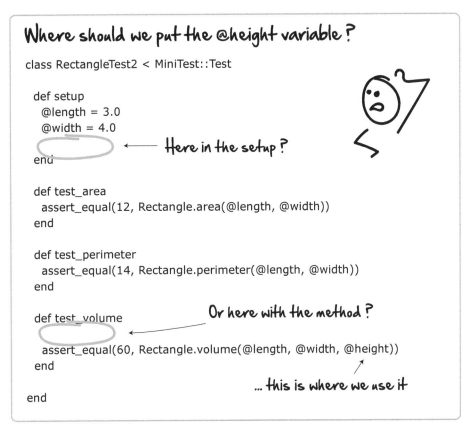

This one's a bit tricky. It is nice to have all the data we want to use captured in the same place at the beginning of the test—in a place like setUp.

```
def setup
  @length = 3.0
  @width = 4.0
  @height = 5.0
end
```

On the other hand, we also like to group data close to the tests that use it. Because area and perimeter calculations don't need height, we could also leave it down here.

```
def test_volume
  @height = 5.0
  assert_equal(60, RectangleCalculator.volume(@length, @width, @height))
end
```

These are the kinds of trade-offs and decisions you are constantly going to be making when writing tests—where to stick your data. Here's a good rule of thumb:

 Group data as close as you can to the tests that are going to be using it.

In this case I would probably keep the @height in the test_volume test and then pull it up into setup as soon as other tests start to want to use it. But not until then.

Alright. Next let's take a look at the power of grouping things by context.

The Clarity of Context

When you first start out, there are going to be some natural ways of grouping tests that just make sense for you and your project.

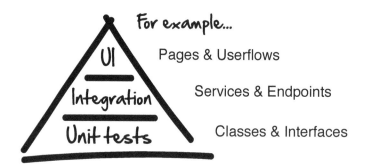

Pages, for example, are a nice way to group UI tests. Services and endpoints are natural points of integration. And 1:1 mappings between classes and tests are already a common convention with unit tests.

There are times, however, when you may get a test with lots of permutations and combinations, and you just need some alternative ways of organizing them.

Take this login page for example. Here are some good tests that test Dave's LoginPage.

```
class LoginPageTest < MiniTest::Test              A little looooooong ...

  def test_authentication_with_valid_credentials_should_have_signout_link
  end

  def test_authentication_with_invalid_credentials_should_not_have_error_message
  end

  def test_authentication_with_valid_credentials_should_have_correct_title
  end

  def test_authentication_with_invalid_credentials_should_have_signin_link
  end

  def test_authentication_with_invalid_credentials_should_have_error_message
  end

end
```

What could we do to make this easier to read?

The tests are good. Each one individually is easy to read. But as we start to get more and more combinations, it's going to get harder and harder to see what's going on.

Pause and pretend this was your code for a second. What would you do to improve the readability or organization of these tests?

Three ways we could improve the organization of these tests :

1. _____

2. _____

3. _____

Well, the first thing you could do is to simply group the related tests together.

Group like things together

```
class LoginPageTest

  # valid credentials

  def test_authentication_with_valid_credentials_should_have_signout_link
  end

  def test_authentication_with_valid_credentials_should_have_correct_title
  end

  # invalid credentials

  def test_authentication_with_invalid_credentials_should_not_have_error_message
  end

  def test_authentication_with_invalid_credentials_should_have_signin_link
  end

  def test_authentication_with_invalid_credentials_should_have_error_message
  end

end
```

Grouping like-minded tests together immediately reduces the mental overload necessary to understand this test and what is going on. And if we wanted to clarify things even further, we could drop in a comment or two just to make the groupings pop a bit more.

What else could we do?

Well, if we look closely at the name of each test, we'd see that the word authentication is repeated a lot. Meaning it's probably safe to assume that all these tests have to do with authentication.

Why don't we make that more clear, and put the word authentication right into the name of the test itself? Like this:

Make the context explicit

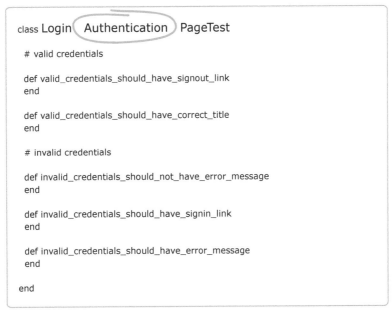

What we are doing here is making the context of the test explicit. Anyone reading this test now knows that all these tests have to do with LoginPageAuthentication, and if they are wanting to add any more tests related to that, they should do so here.

Grouping by context, and making that context explicit, are just two simple things you can do to make your tests easier to organize and easier to read.

And some frameworks, like RSpec, even take this concept further by letting you embed the context of your test in the test itself.

Embed the context

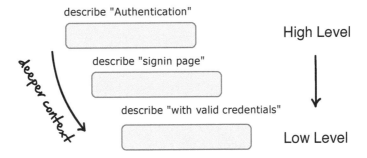

That's what's going on in RSpec when you see tests written like this:

```
describe "Authentication" do
  describe "signin page" do
      describe "with valid credentials" do
      describe "with invalid credentials" do
```

This way of describing your tests, by progressively embedding the context, is handy because it lets you define specific scenarios, and then punch out and write test cases for them when you need to.

Here we can add a new authentication test page easily by simply grouping it with the Authentication context already set up there.

```
describe "Authentication" do
  describe "signin page" do
      describe "with valid credentials" do
      describe "with invalid credentials" do

  describe "new super secret page" do
      describe "with valid credentials" do
      describe "with invalid credentials" do
```

The way to read these tests is to combine all the describe keywords into one sentence like this:

```
describe "Authentication signin page with valid credentials"
describe "Authentication signin page with invalid credentials"
describe "Authentication new super secret page with valid credentials"
describe "Authentication new super secret page with invalid credentials"
```

Organizing our tests like this not only makes our tests easier to read, it makes it easier to:

- Spot bugs
- Find patterns
- See missing test cases

And when we bring it all together in a full-on RSpec test, the result looks something like this:

```
require 'spec_helper'

describe "Authentication" do

  subject { page }

  describe "signin page" do
    before { visit signin_path }

    it { should have_content('Sign in') }
    it { should have_title('Sign in') }
  end
```

```ruby
describe "signin" do
  before { visit signin_path }

  describe "with valid information" do
    let(:user) { FactoryGirl.create(:user) }

    before do
      fill_in "Email",    with: user.email.upcase
      fill_in "Password", with: user.password
      click_button "Sign in"
    end

    it { should have_title(user.name) }
    it { should have_link('Sign out', href: signout_path) }
    it { should_not have_link('Sign in', href: signin_path) }

    describe "followed by signout" do
      before { click_link "Sign out" }
      it { should have_link('Sign in') }
    end
  end

  describe "with invalid information" do
    before { click_button "Sign in" }

    it { should have_title('Sign in') }
    it { should have_error_message('Invalid') }

    describe "after visiting another page" do
      before { click_link "Home" }
      it { should_not have_selector('div.alert.alert-error') }
    end
  end

end

end
```

Now just to be clear, you're not going to need all these fancy ways of organizing tests when you first start out. Start simply by creating one file for each set of tests. It doesn't need to be much more complicated than that.

But just be aware that you have options. And as your test suite grows, know that there are alternatives to grouping and organizing tests other than what you see before you. Experiment. Try things out, and trust your gut when it tells you this feels right and this feels wrong.

And don't sweat it if you aren't using RSpec. The tool isn't important—it's the concept that counts. You can always get away with using much simpler tools like directories and filenames for organizing your tests too.

```
Tests/LoginPage/Authentication/ValidCredentialsTest.rb
Tests/LoginPage/Authentication/InvalidCredentialsTest.rb
```

> ### Money Out the Window
>
> I was on a team once that really got bit from not keeping its tests separated. The team members were using an automated test framework called FIT, which conveniently read data from an Excel spreadsheet and then fed the numbers into the system to be tested.
>
> I have nothing against FIT, but one of the challenges with FIT and these other table-based data entry systems is it makes it easy for teams to add more data, without thinking about how that data should be grouped or separated.
>
> After doing this for several months, the team was in a real bind. The FIT tests were valuable, because they caught important financial calculation bugs from ever entering the system. But they were also a nightmare to maintain because of the amount of time it took testers to figure out which data went with which tests, and how not to break all the tests and data with every little change to the system.
>
> Be wary of tools and frameworks that encourage you to generate lots of data and tests. They can seem like a good idea at the time, but most of the time you don't need them. Instead just write a simple, clear, focused test case for the scenario you want to test and understand, and drop the endless rows of data.
>
> Your tests will be much clearer. Your concerns more isolated. And your tests less brittle and easier to understand.

 Group related tests by context to make them easier to read and support.

Good stuff. Let's try organizing some tests now and see how this works in action.

Intruder Alert

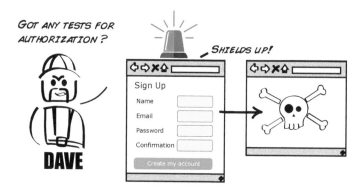

Whoa! Some hackers are trying to access the website, and Dave would like to add some authorization tests in a hurry. The good news is the tests are already written. The bad news is he doesn't know where to put them!

Should we add them to our existing page tests? Or put them into their own new test file focused purely on authorization?

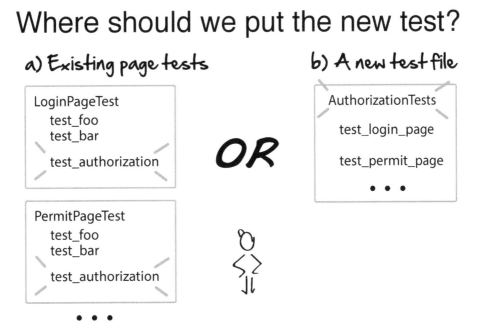

The automatic response most people give in a situation like this is to go with option a), add the new tests to the existing ones already there.

The reason for this is ease. It would be easy to just add a couple authorization tests to the end of each page file and be done with it. Life would go on. And we would probably be fine.

But option b), putting all the authorization tests in a single file, has some merit too. The beauty of grouping all the authorization tests together into one file is that if we ever want to see how authorization for the website works, we've got all the tests in one place.

It's also easier to add new authorization tests, and to note any exceptions or patterns because you have all the authorization tests in one place.

So what's the right answer? That's up to you. In this case I would probably group the authorization tests together into their own test suite. But understand, there is no one way to do this stuff. You are free to group and organize your tests however you like. Just because you are currently doing it one way doesn't mean you can't experiment and try something else.

The point of this exercise isn't that there is a right or wrong answer here. It's to show that you have options and that sometimes grouping things by context, instead of by the functionality, is one way to go.

What We've Learned So Far

This was a slightly more advanced chapter, but I think you were up for it. Once you start writing tests on your own, you will start to develop your own feeling and rules of thumb around what grouping strategies make sense for your project and which don't.

The big takeaway from this chapter is that how you organize your tests makes a big difference in your ability to change them, that there is no one way, and you've got lots of options. So don't be afraid to try different things and to mix things up.

However, these two things will definitely help:

- Keep your tests focused and isolated—and don't try to test too many things at once.
- Group similar tests by context, as it's much easier on your brain.

With this under our belt, we are now ready for our final push. In the next two chapters we are going to look at some of the finer points of unit testing, like how to write tests first. And how to deal with a phenomenon automated testers at all levels of the pyramid face—something known as coupling.

CHAPTER 11

Effective Mocking

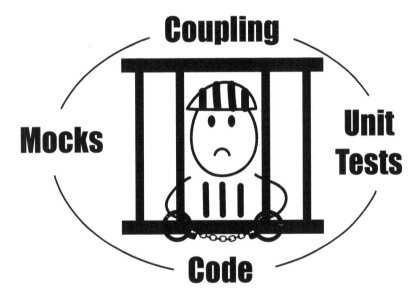

Mocking is an effective tool for unit testing code, but it can be overused. Too many of the wrong kinds of mocks can make your tests brittle and hard to maintain. But the right kind of mocks can give you confidence while simultaneously enabling you to change your designs.

In this chapter we are going to look at the pros and cons that come with this style of unit testing, and see how you can use mocks effectively. By the end of the chapter you'll not only know where the perils of mocking lie, you'll know how to avoid them and make mocks work for you in your code.

Developers, this chapter is on unit testing and is directly focused on you. Testers, you better come along too, as mocking is a term you will hear often, and it would be good if you understood how these things worked.

Listen to the Music

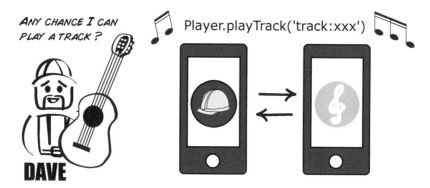

Dave and the team are pumped. Last week they went and saw their favorite band play, The Construction Workers, and then it hit them. What would make their work permit application really shine is the ability to choose which track plays while creating a permit.

So the next week they came up with the following design, tried it, and it worked!

There was just one snag. While testing, they discovered that the connection to the music-streaming service went down periodically. Before the next track would play, the connection would need to be refreshed.

Here is the reconnection logic. What they aren't sure about is how to test it.

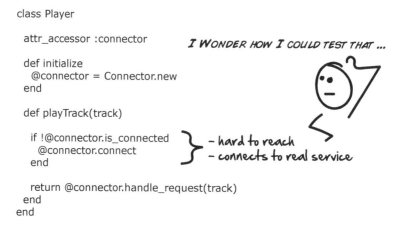

```
class Player

  attr_accessor :connector

  def initialize
    @connector = Connector.new
  end

  def playTrack(track)

    if !@connector.is_connected
      @connector.connect
    end

    return @connector.handle_request(track)
  end
end
```

There is no way from the unit test to control whether the music service is up or down. Even if there was, there's no way of knowing whether @connector.connect got called after, which is what we'd like to know.

This is all too common in unit testing. You have a fix. It's embedded deep in the code. And you have no easy way to get your hands on the code and objects you want to test. It's de-testable (ha!).

In Chapter 12, *Writing Tests First*, on page 199, we'll look at some ways to make our code more testable. But until then, we are in a bit of a pickle. What we need is a way of unit testing that lets us:

- Control and monitor objects deep inside our tests
- While at the same time letting us set up our code to test in specific ways—preferably, without calling the real service

Enter the Mock

Mocks, also sometimes referred to as test doubles,[1] are fake objects we periodically use in automated tests in place of real ones.

Now you may be wondering why on earth we'd ever want to do that. Isn't it always better to test with the real thing? And the answer would normally be yes. Real objects don't lie. They are easier to read. And there's no magic in setting them up—they just work.

But there are occasions when calling the real thing may be problematic. One is when the service you are calling from your unit tests is expensive or slow.

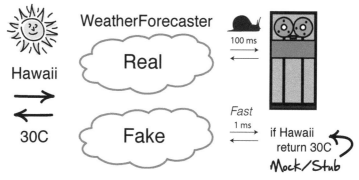

---

1. https://en.wikipedia.org/wiki/Test_double

If you recall from Chapter 6, *Covering Our Bases with Unit Tests*, on page 79, we always want our unit tests to be fast. So any service that is slow or flaky is a good candidate for a mock.

The other occasion is when you have code that is hard to reach.

By being able to drop a mock in, and control and monitor how it works from the outside, you gain a lot of flexibility and power over how you can configure and set up your tests. Not to mention, a mock is a valuable tool for checking whether certain things get done.

Through this lens, let's now return to Dave's example, and see how mocks may be able to help him out.

Step 1: Prepare the Mock

The challenge we face with testing Dave's reconnection logic is we have no way to control what that connector returns when called in the playTrack method.

```
def playTrack(track)
  if !@connector.is_connected
    @connector.connect
  end

  return @connector.handle_request(track)
end
```

The way the code is currently written, the @connector is going to try to connect to the real music service every time it's called, and what we want to do is replace the real @connector object with a fake one—or a mock.

Mocks vs. Stubs

Mocks and stubs are two words you will hear used interchangeably sometimes in automated testing, but they mean two slightly different things.

Stubs are test doubles that return hard-coded data. There's almost no logic to a stub. You simply replace your expensive real-world operation with a hard-coded, stubbed-out fake one and you're done. You just let it do its thing.

```
class StubWeatherForecaster

  def predict_weather(city)
    if city === 'Hawaii'
      return 30
    elsif city === 'Stockholm'
      return 0
    elsif city === 'Winnipeg'
      return -20
    end
  end

end
```

Mocks, on the other hand, not only return data, but they can be remote controlled and monitored.

For example, if you want your weather forecaster to simulate freezing temperatures in Hawaii, or you want to verify that a special humidity calculation got called if the temperature dipped below 0, you could write that with a mock like this:

```
@mockForecaster.expects(:predict_weather).with('Hawaii').returns(-10)
@mockForecaster.expects(:calculate_cold_humidity)
```

If any of these expectations aren't met, the test would fail, proving they never happened.

There aren't any hard-and-fast rules when it comes to choosing mocks or stubs. If all you need is some simple hard-coded data, go with the stub. But if you want to monitor and control, you probably need something more along the lines of a mock.

The most common way to set up test code to be mocked is to inject the objects you want to mock, in through the constructor of the object under test. This is known as *dependency injection.*[2]

The way dependency injection works is you pass in any objects you want to monitor or control, into the object under test via its constructor. By doing that you gain the ability to do two important things:

---

2.   https://en.wikipedia.org/wiki/Dependency_injection

1. Control your mock from the outside in your unit test

2. Monitor, track, and make assertions on the things that happen to your mock as the unit test is run

This is how mocking works. You pass in objects you want to control, and then set expectations on them after.

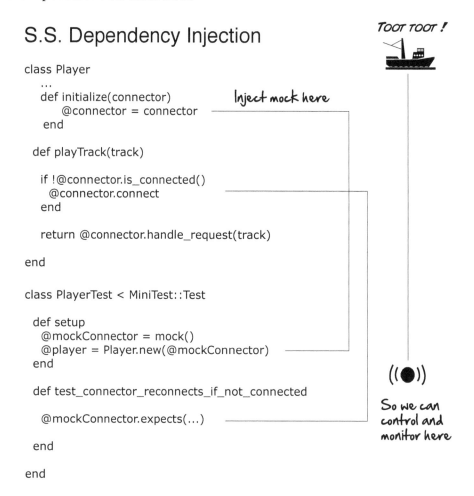

Step 2: Set Expectations

The expectations you set on your mock depend on the scenario you want to test. In our case, we want to verify that @connector.connect gets called in the event the @connector is not connected.

Setting expectations

```ruby
class Player
  ...
  def initialize(connector)
    @connector = connector
  end

  def playTrack(track)

    if !@connector.is_connected()

      @connector.connect

    end

    return @connector.handle_request(track)
  end

class PlayerTest < MiniTest::Test

  def setup
    @mockConnector = mock()
    @player = Player.new(@mockConnector)
  end

  def test_connector_reconnects_if_not_connected
```

I WILL RETURN FALSE

THIS BETTER HAPPEN !!!

(1) `@mockConnector.expects(:is_connected).returns('false')`

(2) `@mockConnector.expects(:connect)`

(3) `@player.playTrack('track:xxx')`
```ruby
  end

end
```

where we set our expectations

We start by first making sure that when playTrack is called on Player, the @connector.is_connected returns false. We cover that with this line here:

```ruby
@mockConnector.expects(:is_connected).returns(false)
```

Next, we want to ensure that @connector.connect is called. This is the basis of our test, and how we will know the reconnection logic is working. We cover that with this line here:

```ruby
@mockConnector.expects(:connect)
```

Then thirdly, we need a line of code to make it all go and kick the whole thing off. And that's this line here:

```
@player.playTrack('track:xxx')
```

When we bring it all together, we have a nice little test that ensures our reconnection logic is called, all without talking to the real music service.

```
class PlayerTest < MiniTest::Test

  def setup
    @mockConnector = mock()
    @player = Player.new(@mockConnector)
  end

  def test_connector_reconnects_if_not_connected
    @mockConnector.expects(:is_connected).returns(false)
    @mockConnector.expects(:connect)
    @player.playTrack('track:xxx')
  end

end
```

And that's how mocking works! You inject your objects, set their expectations, and then verify they happen.

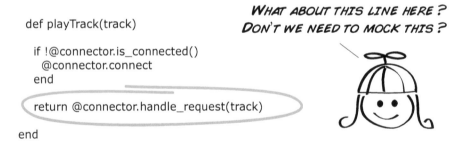

Ah—good question! There are two types of mocking frameworks out there. Those that are *strict* and those that are *loose*.

Strict mocking frameworks are those that make you explicitly write out every call to every mock in your test—whether you are testing them or not. So if you were using a strict mocking framework, you would indeed need to include that line in your test case—else it would complain and fail.

Loose mocking frameworks, on the other hand, are much more forgiving. So long as the expectation on the mocks you set is met, the test will be happy.

Loose mocks are the most popular of the two today. By keeping a mock loose, the intent of your test is made clearer (less noise), your code is less brittle (less coupling—more on this shortly), and your test suites in general are easier to maintain (more joy).

But good question. My recommendation is to keep it loose.

Now with all this wonderful mocking knowledge under your belt, you may be tempted to rush out and start mocking all those annoying dependencies you've got in your test cases.

But before you do, stick around and see what happens when Dave and crew do exactly that, and witness the challenges we face when we start heavily mocking our code.

The Shackles of Coupling

Having a senior engineer like Erik join the team had an immediate impact on the direction and spirit of our automated tests. Not only was Erik a wealth of knowledge about design and testing, he helped us look at our code in a new light and with a fresh set of eyes. Which is why we all stood up and listened when he said:

Too many unit tests? What? How is that even possible? We had been under the impression there was no such thing as too many tests. What could possibly go wrong by adding more tests!?

He then proceeded to draw a picture and started to explain this term we had heard of but never fully understood—something called *coupling*.

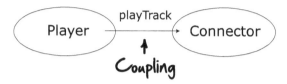

Coupling is the degree with which two objects are connected. When our Player object calls a method on our Connector object, those objects become coupled. We can't change one without also changing the other.

Now all programs require some degree of coupling. If there were no coupling, our objects wouldn't be able to speak to each other. Nothing would happen.

But one thing we *do* try to avoid when building systems is over-coupling our objects and systems together. Because the more coupled things are, the harder things become to change. That's why we only speak to objects through their public APIs, and leave their internal data and methods to themselves.

Now where things get interesting is when you bring unit tests into the mix, because unit tests are a form of coupling too.

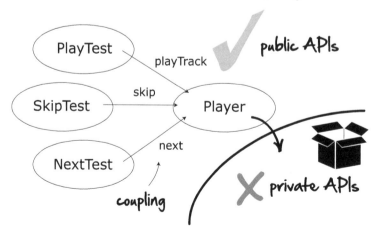

So long as we keep it high level and stick to the public APIs of our objects, we are generally OK. Not too much coupling.

 Test the public APIs of your objects. Not the internal private ones.

But look what happens once our designs start to get a little more complicated, and we continue to expose the internals of our objects in our tests. Coupling city!

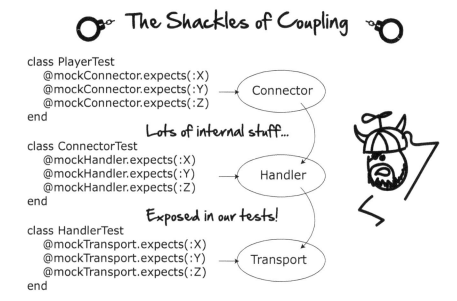

Now not only are our objects coupled together, but so are the mocks, their expectations, and our tests! Too much coupling. It's all locked in.

And if we continue this pattern and get lazy with our design, it won't be long before we all end up in a place no developer ever wants to go. The Swamp of Mocking.

The Swamp of Mocking

The Swamp of Mocking is where unit test codebases go that have been so completely overrun by mocks that the original tests don't even make sense anymore.

```
class LoginServiceTest < MiniTest::Test

  def setup
    @mockRoles = mock()
    @mockPermissions = mock()
    @mockAuthorization = mock()
    @mockAuthentication = mock()
    @mockAnalytics = mock()
    @mockDatabaseAdapter = mock()
    @mockMainFrame = mock()
    @mockLogging = mock()

    @login_service = LoginService.new(@mockRoles, @mockPermissions,
            @mockAuthorization, @mockAuthentication,@mockAnalytics,
            @mockDatabaseAdapter, @mockMainFrame, @mockLogging)
  end

  def test_valid_login
    @mockRoles.expects(:check_role)
    @mockPermissions.expects(:check_permissions)
    @mockAuthorization.expects(:authorize)
    @mockAuthentication.expects(:authenticate)
    @mockAnalytics.expects(:record_login)
    @mockDatabaseAdapter.expects(:connect)
    @mockMainFrame.expects(:predict_weather)
    @mockLogging.expects(:log)

    @login_service.login('username', 'password')

  end

end
```

x10,000 lines of setup

x15,000 lines of verification

one line of test

You'll know you are in the Swamp of Mocking when:

- You have more lines of mock, expectation, and setup than actual test code.

- Every time you go to make a change, you back out because the change would be too painful because of all the coupling and tests it would break.

- You have no idea what the original intent of the test was.

Life is tough in the swamp. The very tests that were meant to speed you up end up instead hurting you and slowing you down. There is so much noise, you can no longer make heads or tails of what the tests are supposed to do. You only know that every time you go to make a change, something breaks. And improving the design ends up being painful. So you don't.

Now to be fair, this isn't just a mocking problem. It's a design problem. Classes with this amount of coupling between objects and tests are going to be hard to maintain no matter what.

But mocking-style unit tests seem drawn to the Swamp of Mocking more than others, and if you aren't careful how you use your mocks, they'll end up using you and you'll end up here before you know it.

Fortunately, there is a way of using mocks that doesn't require this amount of coupling. It involves sticking to only testing the surface of your objects, and leaving the details inside alone.

Ports and Adapters

Ports-and-adapters[3] is a software architecture that encourages you to separate the core functionality of your application from any external boundaries or services.

A port or adapter is typically an external service like a web server, but it could equally be a call to any external service, or even the input stream from your keyboard. Anything that is an input or an output to your system could be a candidate.

The beauty of thinking about your software this way is it lets you take a much more black box–style approach to your testing. Instead of aggressively testing all the internals of your systems (and coupling everything together), you stick to the surface and instead focus more on the inputs and outputs.

Ports and Adapters

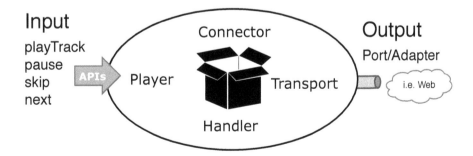

---

3.   http://www.dossier-andreas.net/software_architecture/ports_and_adapters.html

Kind of, yes. Think about it like this. We could mock and test every interaction of every method, and have an extremely coupled, highly tested system that would work, but would be nearly impervious to change.

Or, we could forget the internals, test our system from the outside in, and simply mock the one thing we don't want our unit tests talking to—the outside world. In this case, a music service.

Mock the external ports and adapters

Player ← FakeTransport

Use real objects

Connector   Handler

Mock or Stub here!

FakeTransport
```
if valid_track
return { "success" : "true" }
if invalid_track
return { "success" : "false" }
```

By mocking or stubbing the Transport (the object responsible for communicating with the outside world), we can do all sorts of things.

We can echo back server errors. We can simulate disconnects. All while using real Connector and Handler objects inside.

Here's the hardcoded `FakeTransport` stub that would return canned responses to certain predetermined tests:

```
class FakeTransport

  def send(uri)
    if uri == 'valid_track'
      return true;
    end

    if uri == 'invalid_track'
      return false;
    end

  end
end
```

And here's the dependency-injected `Player` object and tests. Testing would happen if a good or a bad track request is sent to the music server.

```
class PlayerStubTest < MiniTest::Test

  def setup
    @fakeTransport = FakeTransport.new
    @player = Player.new(@fakeTransport)
  end

  def test_can_play_valid_track
    assert @player.playTrack('valid_track')
  end

  def test_fails_with_invalid_track
    assert !@player.playTrack('invalid_track')
  end

end
```

Taking this more black box[4] approach to unit testing has a number of other advantages:

Take a more black box approach to testing

+ Real objects
+ Less coupling
+ Easier to change
+ Better coverage
+ Fewer bugs

---

4. https://en.wikipedia.org/wiki/Black-box_testing

1. Getting to work with real objects

    Real objects are always preferable to mocks because real objects don't
    lie. They reflect how the system is going to behave at runtime (meaning
    production). So there is no danger of setting up the mock incorrectly in
    a test and then having it blow up in production.

2. Way less coupling

    Coupling is the killer of change. By testing our objects from the outside
    in, and looking at our systems as more of black boxes, our tests are way
    less coupled to our code, which makes our designs easier to change.

3. Easier to change

    This is so important it bears repeating. As you gain more understanding
    and insight into how your code works, you are going to want to change
    it. Writing tests without a whole bunch of highly invasive mocks lets you
    do that.

4. Better coverage

    Outside-in tests exercise our object models from end-to-end—not just the
    one layer down from the object we are testing. This gives better end-to-
    end coverage while exercising the code closer to how it's going to behave
    in production.

5. Fewer bugs—better tests

    Black box–style tests don't suffer from the overhead and setup the way
    heavily mocked tests do. There is way less swamp here. The tests are
    generally easier to read, easier to maintain, and more fun to write because
    they test stuff we care about, like what our objects do.

It may be hard to see in this trivial example, but mocking your tests with
ports and adapters is a powerful testing technique.

Once you know where the ports and adapters are in your system, and you
realize you can mock them out, you can come up with some powerful testing
infrastructure that not only gives you great confidence in your tests, but also
enables you to update and change your design.

And if you can pull that off, that's a pretty neat trick.

Alright. Let's open up the microphone to the floor and see if people have any
questions for discussion.

There Is Nothing Like the Real Thing

 I once almost broke a whole bunch of Spotify car integrations because of my overuse of mocking. I was adding the ability to save the currently playing track to the user's playlist. I thought I had my bases covered by testing the various permutations and combinations of IDs and tracks in my mocks.

I was wrong.

Only by doing some last-minute gut checking on some actual physical car devices did I realize my mistake. And of course it was the afternoon before a Swedish long weekend, which means nobody was around.

I learned three good lessons that day.

One. If you are not sure your feature is 100% correct, it's always good to do a sanity check on real physical devices.

Two. Favor real objects over fake ones. If I had taken the time to write my code against the real thing and not taken the easy way out and used the fakes, I would have caught this bug much earlier and saved myself a lot of stress and running around.

But perhaps most important is three. Never check in big sweeping changes just before a long weekend.

Open Mic

> BY HARD-CODING THE SERVER RESPONSES INTO FAKE TRANSPORT, AREN'T YOU JUST SWAPPING ONE FORM OF COUPLING FOR ANOTHER !?

Yes! You are absolutely right. By hard-coding the server response into the stub itself, we have now introduced another form of coupling between the server and the unit tests. If the server response changes, we need to update our unit tests accordingly. Coupling isn't just for objects. We can have coupling between systems and data too.

Here is a table summarizing the main differences between these two approaches, which Martin Fowler refers to as the *Classicist* vs. *Mockist* approach to unit testing.[5]

Classicist vs Mockist

Classicist	Mockist
Likes real objects	Prefers fake
Uses mocks occasionally to test collaborations, ports, and adapters	Uses mocks all the time
Will hard-code collaborations	Will mock collaborations
Tests more coarse grained - more integration style tests	Tests more fine grained - may miss integrations
Don't couple tests to implementation	Mockists do
Don't like thinking about implementation when writing tests	Mockists do
Don't mind creating query methods to support testing	Mockists typically don't have to

> YOU MAKE IT SOUND LIKE MOCKING IS REALLY BAD. ARE YOU SAYING WE SHOULD NEVER MOCK?

No. Not at all. Mocking and dependency injection are great tools for helping us write good test code. Without mocks, and the ability to inject ourselves deeply into certain places in our code, testing certain collaborations would be really, really hard.

But...if there is one thing I want you to walk away from in this chapter, it's that you don't have to mock. And it's often better to stick with testing with plain old objects when you can instead.

5. http://martinfowler.com/articles/mocksArentStubs.html

WHAT IF THERE IS AN INTERNAL METHOD I WANT TO TEST... BUT IT'S NOT PART OF THE PUBLIC INTERFACE. HOW SHOULD I GO ABOUT TESTING THAT?

Whoa—good question. Usually the best thing to do there is to always see if you can test the private methods through one of your public interfaces.

Testing it this way ensures that the method will be exercised in the same way that your clients will use it. And if you can't trigger that method via one of your public interfaces, maybe you don't need it in the first place.

WHAT, IF ANYTHING, IS THE BIG TAKEAWAY HERE FOR US TESTERS?

The takeaway for testers here is that coupling is something we need to deal with in tests, just like developers need to deal with it in code.

For example, when we write UI tests, we are coupling our tests to that user interface. So if the UI changes, so do our tests. This is why it's sometimes best to hold off on writing UI tests until the UI has gone through a lot of iterations and finally settled down. No sense in coupling prematurely before we need to.

With integration tests, and the testing of our web services, we have the same thing, only here we are coupled to responses from web servers and the data they return. But we are coupled nonetheless.

The other big one, which we haven't really gotten into, is data. Test data is a form of coupling too. If your tests expect certain data to be there when they run, the tests and the data are coupled. You can't do one without the other.

So coupling is everywhere in automated testing, and we need to be careful how we manage it. Some coupling is always inevitable. But where we can, we like to reduce it. Because the more we couple, the less our software is open to change.

What We've Learned So Far

Wow. That was a tricky chapter. We got into some pretty deep stuff there, and if all of that doesn't make a lot of sense, don't worry. It only took me ten years to wrap my head around some of these ideas, and if you understood half of what we covered here, you are way ahead of me when I was in your shoes.

But here are a few key takeaways for the chapter:

- Unit tests don't have to be mocks. You can (and should) prefer to work with real objects instead.

- By limiting your unit tests to the public APIs of your objects, and by testing your objects from the outside in, you can reduce coupling, making your objects more open to design, and easier to change.

- Mocks are a handy tool, but try not to overuse them. They are great for dealing with tricky, hard-to-program scenarios, but they can be abused. So try to stay out of the swamp.

- As much as you can, focus your unit tests on external behavior (not internal object mechanics). Coupling is the killer. The more you can test from the outside in, the easier your tests and design will be to maintain and change.

Phew. Do you have the energy for one more? In the last chapter on TDD, we are going to look at one final technique for writing unit tests that can help developers get going when they are at a loss for what to test and aren't quite sure how to begin.

So hop on the bus for one more stop. Let's wrap things up by learning about the mind-bending powers that come with writing tests first.

CHAPTER 12

Writing Tests First

Knowing what to test can be a real challenge. There is no magic line in the sand that tells you when you've tested enough. There is a lot of complexity—even dealing with simple tasks. And there's no guarantee that whatever you produce will be of good design. In short, there are a lot of things to master.

But one technique, if properly applied, can help unlock these and other mysteries of the universe. By learning the technique of test-driven development (TDD), you'll learn how to keep your code clean and your solutions simple.

To be sure, writing your tests first is no guarantee of either great code or perfect tests—but it does help deal with complexity while simultaneously keeping you from feeling overwhelmed.

Developers, this chapter is going to give you yet another powerful tool to aid you in writing your unit tests. Testers, you may just want to stick around because even though this chapter focuses on unit testing, the ideas behind it might just contain some food for thought around how you go about writing your tests too. So hang out and stay tuned for the Open Mic section near the end.

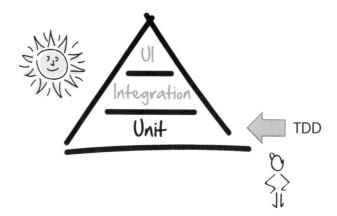

Where to Begin

Dave and his engineers are longing for a style of calculator they used back in the good old days—something they reverently refer to as the RPN or Reverse Polish notation[1] style calculator.

RPN calculators are just like regular old calculators with one key difference. With RPN style calculators you enter your numbers first, and your operations after.

So instead of simply adding two numbers by typing:

$$1 + 2 = 3$$

On an RPN style calculator you would instead type:

---

1.   https://en.wikipedia.org/wiki/Reverse_Polish_notation

Adding two numbers

1 ENTER
2 ENTER
+ ENTER
_____
3 Voila!

Now before we look at how to create this calculator using full-on TDD, let's spend a minute thinking about what kind of unit tests we would like to write. Don't worry about fancy user interfaces or anything like that. Instead, just think about what kind of unit tests you'd like to write for the brains of the calculator using plain old objects.

Write down at least three unit test cases you think you would write to support the adding of two numbers RPN style.

Test cases that would give us confidence we could add two numbers RPN style

1. _____

2. _____

3. _____

Write here

Don't look ahead! This is a chance for you to practice doing TDD in a safe environment. Don't worry, we'll go over the answer soon enough. Go back and give it a go.

If you came up with some tests different than what you see below, congrats! You can add these as an exercise later for practice. But for now, let's start with these three.

Test cases that would give us confidence we could add two numbers RPN style

1. Enter single number

2. Enter two numbers

3. Add two numbers

We are going to write these test first

OK, we are almost ready. Let's first go over the concept of TDD, and then see what it feels like to drive development with Dave's RPN style calculator.

What Is Test-Driven Development (TDD)?

Test-driven development, or TDD, is the practice of writing tests first before adding production code. Now you may be wondering why on earth anyone would want to do that. Isn't it hard enough writing the code regularly and then testing it after? What could we possibly gain by doing this backwards?

Well it turns out that writing tests first helps deal with one of the devils we all need to handle in software—stress.

You see, when we write software, complexity, stress, and a sense of being overwhelmed are never far from our doorstep. And it doesn't take much for even the simplest of tests to quickly spiral out of control and seem daunting.

TDD helps to give you focus. By starting with a single test and ignoring the rest of the outside world, you eliminate and ignore much of the conventional thinking and noise that distracts you from your mission, enabling you to focus on one thing at a time.

The way TDD does this is by working in three distinct steps.

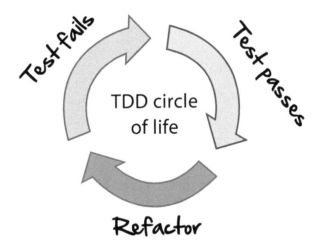

Step 1: Write a Failing Test

In this step you aren't thinking about a solution. Here you are thinking about design. Here you are writing a test to verify that the code you are about to add in the second step works. So here you need to put your design hat on and "think" the API for the code into existence.

Step 2: Make the Test Pass

Here you take off your design hat and get into solution mode. You are now free to do whatever it takes to make the test pass. You can be cheeky and return a hardcoded value simply to make the test pass. Or you can take a bigger step, and implement a more robust solution. It's up to you.

Step 3: Refactor

Arguably the most important step out of the three, and the easiest to forget, refactoring is where you go back over your test and solution and make any necessary adjustments in the spirit of improving your overall design. With the tests at your back, you are now free to make changes.

Here you can extract methods, rename variables, and the like. It's a crucial step because it's here where you really improve your design and make it more maintainable. In step 2, you are making the tests pass. In step 3, you are making them pass in style.

Once you finish with refactoring, you are then free to grab another test and repeat the process all over again. You continue to do this until you can think of no more tests, or your system does everything it needs to do for the scope of this feature.

Advantages of Working This Way

The advantages of working this way, as opposed to testing last or not testing at all, are the following:

1. It helps prevent over-engineering.

   If you apply TDD by the book, you aren't allowed to add any production code until you have a failing test first proving that you need it. This simple act does something remarkable to code. It prevents it from becoming over-engineered.

   XP (extreme programming) has a term called Yagni,[2] or You Ain't Gonna Need It. Meaning before you add that big hairy complex ball of spaghetti to the codebase, can you show me the failing unit test that indicates we need it first? TDD and YAGNI are how XPers keep their code solutions simple and their code humble.

2. It tends to produce better designed, better tested code.

   Because you are thinking about design and testing from the beginning, not only does TDD help prevent over-engineering, it tends to produce code that is simpler to maintain and easier to read—two attributes we'd all like to see more of in our codebases.

3. It helps deal with complexity.

   When you start any new project or feature, there are so many things to check and so many things that can go wrong, that if you don't have a strategy for dealing with the stress, it's easy to feel overwhelmed.

   The beauty of TDD is it helps keep the demon of stress at bay by letting you focus on one test at a time. This simple act greatly simplifies the problem and allows you to focus.

---

2. http://martinfowler.com/bliki/Yagni.html

4. It feels good.

Once you get into the habit of writing your tests first, you will notice a natural rhythm and feel good about the work you're doing. You'll get these quick hits of instant gratification, you'll feel like you're making steady progress forward, and you'll always have a working system as each passing test moves you closer to your goal.

But don't take my word for it. Let's go back to Dave and his calculator and try it out now.

Seeing It in Action

OK. So these are the three test cases we are going to TDD out.

Test cases that would give us confidence we could add two numbers RPN style

1. Enter single number

2. Enter two numbers

3. Add two numbers

We are going to write these test first

We will just take these logically in the order a user would as if they were using the calculator. Let's start with entering a single number.

Step 1: Write a Failing Test

1. Enter a single number

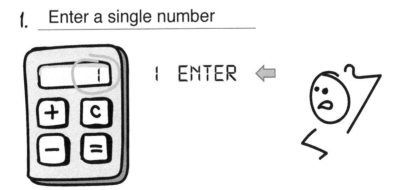

Show time. Time to put your design beret on and see if you can't write a test that does two things:

1. Verifies our calculator can take a single number

2. Then returns the result (which for us will always be the last number added or operated on)

Take a moment and try writing a unit test that could do that.

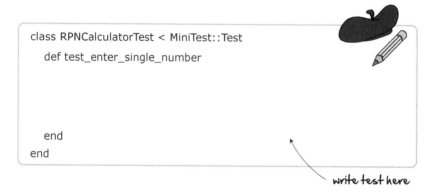

```
class RPNCalculatorTest < MiniTest::Test
    def test_enter_single_number



    end
end
```

write test here

OK. How did that go? Did the code come flowing? Did it pour out of your pencil faster than you could write?

If you are like most of us when we first got into TDD, the answer was probably no. Because you know what? Writing tests first can be kinda hard. And you know why? Complexity.

Even after shutting off the rest of the outside world and focusing on just that one test, look at the sheer number of design decisions to go into writing a single line of code.

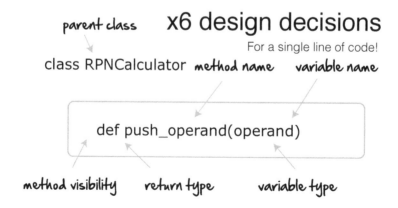

parent class   x6 design decisions

For a single line of code!

class RPNCalculator   method name   variable name

def push_operand(operand)

method visibility   return type   variable type

In order to push a single number into our calculator, we need to think about the following:

- Responsibility—where am I going to put the behavior for this new method?
- Naming—what am I going to call it, and the parent class that is going to hold it?
- Input variables—what am I going to pass this thing as input?
- Output variables—what is it going to return?
- Visibility—is this thing going to be public or private?

Yes—all this for a little line of code. And we haven't even gotten around to actually doing anything yet!

So how do we cut through all this complexity? Easy.

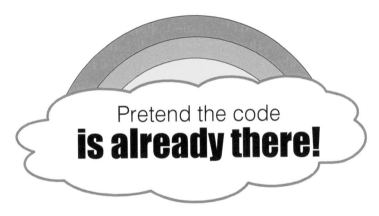

Now you are simply calling it from your test and typing it out.

```ruby
class RPNCalculatorTest < MiniTest::Test
  def test_enter_single_number

    @calculator = Calculator.new
    @calculator.push_operand(1.0)
    assert_equal(1.0, @calculator.result);

  end
end
```

For example, we can pretend that our RPNCalculator class has a method called push_operand that takes an operand (a fancy word for number) and stores it somewhere (we'll worry where in step 2). And that it has another method called result that simply returns the result of the last number pushed. That's it!

When you start to imagine that the code you need already exists, interesting things start to happen:

1. You flip into design mode.

   Test-driven development may start with a "T," but what it's really about is "D," or design. When you write tests first, you are designing your software. That does a couple of things. For one, it gives you exactly what you need—because it's you designing it. And two, you get instant feedback about whether your design is working in the form of a test.

2. You write testable code.

   Testable code in itself isn't the goal—building a great high-quality product for our customers is. But building testable code helps us in getting there. So by thinking about your code in terms of tests, it helps you get closer to these other important things in return.

When we run this test...boom! It fails. It fails because we haven't created the RNPCalculator object yet. Which is good. We always want to start out with a failing test.

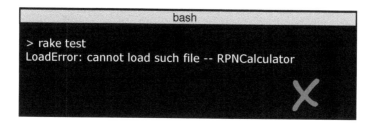

 No production code without first writing a failing test.

Now that we've got one, we are ready to make it pass.

Step 2: Make It Pass

This is where to take off our design beret and flip back into engineering mode. Here we are thinking of nothing else other than how best to make this test pass.

The goal here isn't to build and design everything. It's to build just enough to get this test to pass. Now that's a very subjective statement. Let me explain.

There's a school of thought in TDD that recommends always doing the simplest thing possible when making a test pass. If you took that literally, you might choose just to store that number as a variable RPNCalculator class, and then return it as part of the result like this.

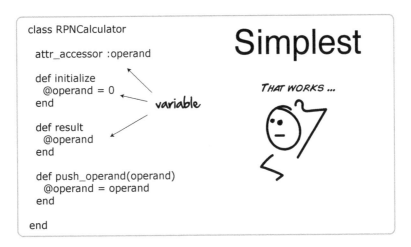

This is a perfectly valid way to get our test to pass. And it's probably the simplest thing we can code (returning hardcoded 0 from result would be even simpler).

But if we look ahead a bit, we know long term that this solution isn't going to cut it. What we really want is something a bit more heavy—like a Stack or an Array. Something capable of supporting multiple numbers.

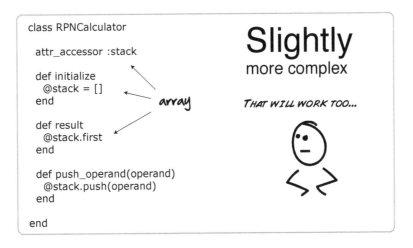

Now you may be wondering—why would we ever want to go for the first solution over the second? The answer is most times you wouldn't. You would almost always go with number two.

Except when you get into trouble.

When TDDers get stuck, they sometimes find it handy to "gear down." Gearing down means committing whatever sins are necessary to get the current test to pass. And then once it's passing, go back in and look for the real solution after.

Think of it like the gears in a big 4x4 truck climbing a mountain. If the road is clear, you can see exactly where you are going, kick it into high gear, drop in the obvious solution, and feel free to race ahead.

So usually you would go with the obvious solution. But when the obvious solution isn't there, don't be afraid to gear down.

Another way to stay out of the mud is to always refactor.

Step 3: Refactor

Refactoring is where we go over all the code we've recently written, and see if there is any way we can improve our design.

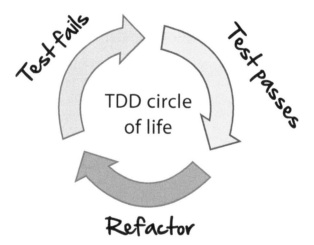

Unfortunately, there's not much for us to improve at this point in our journey. We haven't written much code and everything looks pretty clean. But we'll be refactoring something shortly in the next couple tests.

OK. So that's one pass through the TDD cycle of life. Let's turn the crank again quickly and add that second and third test.

Cycle, Rinse, Repeat

OK, here is test number two. This is just like test number one, except now we want to enter two numbers in our calculator, and ensure that the second number is the one that would show up on our display.

First step is to write a failing test.

Step 1: Write failing test

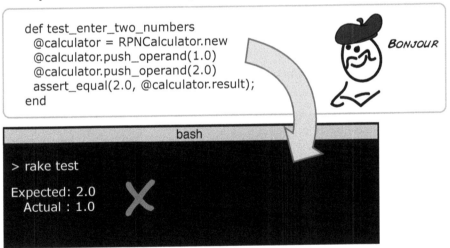

```
def test_enter_two_numbers
  @calculator = RPNCalculator.new
  @calculator.push_operand(1.0)
  @calculator.push_operand(2.0)
  assert_equal(2.0, @calculator.result);
end
```

```
bash
> rake test

Expected: 2.0
  Actual : 1.0
```

OK, good. We've got our failing test. Now we just need to make it pass. Which we can by instead returning the last element added to our array and not the first. Like this.

Step 2: Make it pass

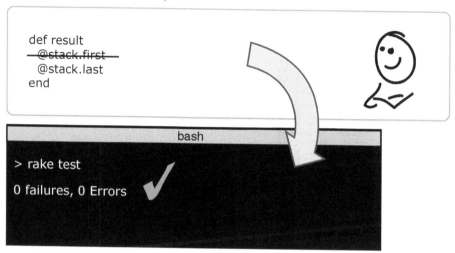

```
def result
  @stack.first
  @stack.last
end
```

```
                              bash
> rake test
0 failures, 0 Errors  ✓
```

Now we are ready to refactor, which we can do by pulling out some common setup code into its own method.

Step 3: Refactor

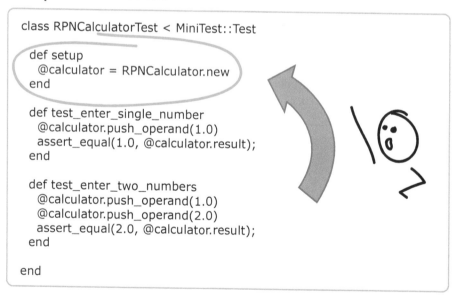

```
class RPNCalculatorTest < MiniTest::Test

  def setup
    @calculator = RPNCalculator.new
  end

  def test_enter_single_number
    @calculator.push_operand(1.0)
    assert_equal(1.0, @calculator.result);
  end

  def test_enter_two_numbers
    @calculator.push_operand(1.0)
    @calculator.push_operand(2.0)
    assert_equal(2.0, @calculator.result);
  end

end
```

OK. That wasn't so bad. Two down. One to go. Here comes test number three. This is the one where we actually add our two numbers.

3. Add two numbers

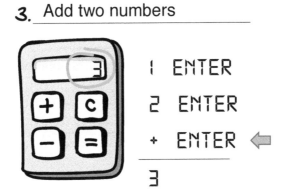

Let's start again with the test.

Step 1: Test

```ruby
class RPNCalculatorTest < MiniTest::Test

  def test_add_two_numbers
    @calculator.push_operand(1.0)
    @calculator.push_operand(2.0)

    @calculator.???

    assert_equal(3.0, @calculator.result);
  end

end
```

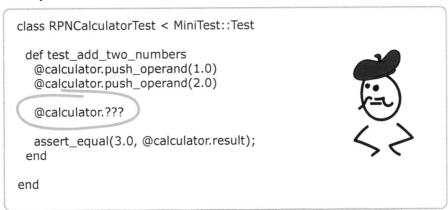

The code we need to add two numbers doesn't exist yet. We need to create it.

This is the most fun part of TDD (actually it's all pretty fun). Because here you get to manifest and pull from the universe whatever it is you need to make the adding of two numbers a reality. It's like magic.

Imagine the code you want to use already exists. You are simply going to use it. Here are a few options to get you going.

Creative Design Mode

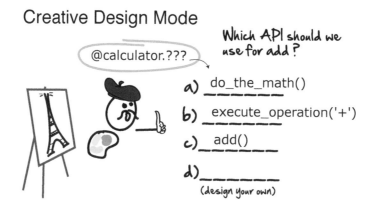

The do_the_math method is probably a little too ambiguous for our taste. execute_operation holds promise, as we can probably expect a plus sign to come at us eventually somewhere in the program.

But the simplest one we can go with for now is probably calling our newly created method add. So let's go with this for now.

Step 1: Write failing test

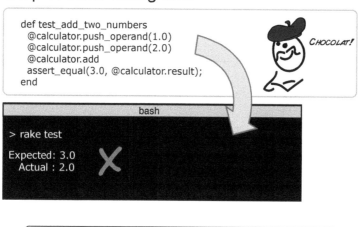

Ah ha! Great question. As you start writing tests, you are inevitably going to discover some new ones. What you can do in these cases is write the new test cases down either on a pad of paper, or as TODO comments at the end of your test first. Like these.

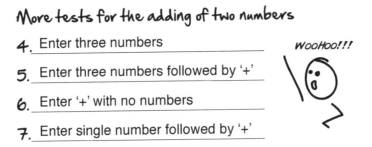

More tests for the adding of two numbers

4. Enter three numbers
5. Enter three numbers followed by '+'
6. Enter '+' with no numbers
7. Enter single number followed by '+'

WooHoo!!!

That way when you finish whatever test it is you are currently working on, you can come back and handle any new test cases. So don't be afraid to keep a notepad nearby ready to jot things down.

Here's one way we could go about adding two numbers in our add method.

Step 2: Make it pass

```
def add
    # pop the first number
    first = stack.pop

    # pop the second number
    second = stack.pop

    # add them together
    result = first + second

    # push the result back on the stack
    @stack.push(result)
  end

end
```

```
bash
> rake test
0 failures, 0 Errors  ✓
```

Here we simply pop each number off the stack, add them together, and then push the result back on. That would do it. And all our tests would pass.

But don't sip that cocktail just yet. Remember, we always need to go back and do that last crucial step, refactoring, to see if there is anything we could improve in our design.

Step 3: Refactor

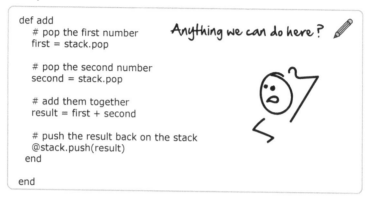

As nicely as this code reads, we could clean up a few things in here. One refactoring we could do is inline the first and second variables.

Step 3: Refactor (cont')

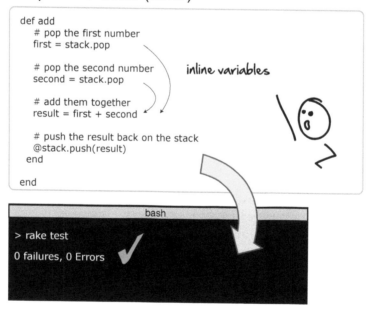

By inlining these two variables right into result, we can shave off a few lines of code and make things a little easier to read.

Step 3: Refactor (cont')

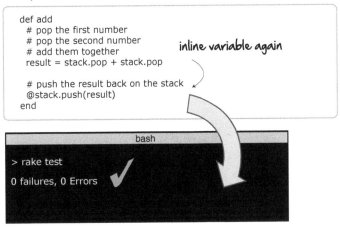

Here we can do this same trick again, only this time we can inline the result itself into the @stack.push operation like this.

Step 3: Refactor (cont')

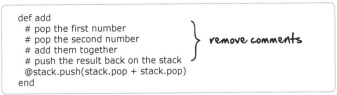

This is looking good. All we need to do is clean up some leftover comments.

Step 3: Refactor (cont')

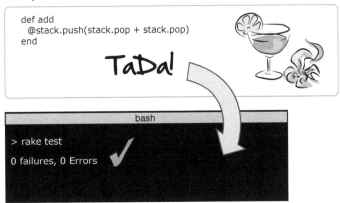

And voila! We have some nicely refactored, easy-to-read code!

I can't over emphasize the importance of this last refactoring step. It's the one that's the most difficult to remember, and the one you are most likely to skip and gloss over too. So make a sticky. Put it on your monitor. And remember.

Also notice how we ran the tests after each stage of our refactoring? That's something you are going to want to get into the habit of doing. That way you'll know instantly when you've broken something.

Here's the final product, including unit tests for all those new ones we discovered along the way. Here are the unit tests:

cswp/test/models/calculator/rpn_calculator_test.rb
```ruby
require 'test_helper'
require 'calculator/rpn_calculator'

class RPNCalculatorTest < MiniTest::Test

  def setup
    @calculator = RPNCalculator.new
  end

  def test_enter_single_number
    @calculator.push_operand(1.0)
    assert_equal(1.0, @calculator.result);
  end

  def test_enter_two_numbers
    @calculator.push_operand(1.0)
    @calculator.push_operand(2.0)
    assert_equal(2.0, @calculator.result);
  end
```

```
def test_add_two_numbers
  @calculator.push_operand(1.0)
  @calculator.push_operand(2.0)
  @calculator.add
  assert_equal(3.0, @calculator.result);
end

def test_entering_threenumbers
  @calculator.push_operand(1.0)
  @calculator.push_operand(2.0)
  @calculator.push_operand(99.0)
  assert_equal(99.0, @calculator.result);
end

def test_entering_threenumbers_followed_by_a_plus
  @calculator.push_operand(1.0)
  @calculator.push_operand(2.0)
  @calculator.push_operand(3.0)
  @calculator.add
  assert_equal(5.0, @calculator.result);
end

def test_entering_plus_with_no_numbers
  @calculator.add
  assert_equal(0.0, @calculator.result);
end

def test_enter_single_number_followed_by_plus
  @calculator.push_operand(1.0)
  @calculator.add
  assert_equal(1.0, @calculator.result);
end

end
```

And here is our handy dandy RPN calculator:

cswp/app/models/calculator/rpn_calculator.rb
```
class RPNCalculator

  attr_accessor :stack

  def initialize
    @stack = []
  end

  def result
    if @stack.count == 0
      return 0.0
    end
    @stack.last
  end

  def push_operand(operand)
    @stack.push(operand)
```

```
  end

  def add
    if @stack.count > 1
      @stack.push(stack.pop + stack.pop)
    end
  end

end
```

Alright. So we covered a lot there. Let's go to the mic and see if we can't now take a few questions from the audience.

Open Mic

That depends on what you mean by up-front design. If you mean going off into the Himalayas and thinking about how you are going to design your system for six months, then yes.

But there's nothing wrong with stopping and thinking about your design, or collaborating with peers on how you'd like to build something.

TDD isn't an excuse to hack or not think. What it is there for is to give you a sandbox to quickly try your designs out on real production code.

TDDers are always suspicious of designs or architecture diagrams that haven't been touched by code. So while they aren't against doing some upfront thinking about how they'd like to go about designing things, they don't really trust their designs until they see them running in working code.

That gives them the confidence that their designs are going to work and their abstractions are fit for purpose. But good question.

HOW DOES *TDD* RELATE TO THE OTHER LEVELS OF THE PYRAMID?
FOR EXAMPLE, SHOULD *I* BE DOING *TDD* WITH MY *UI* TESTS?

Here's the thing. TDD as a concept is super handy. Whenever you need to add a new feature, or fix a new bug, thinking about what success looks like before you actually do the work helps define success, limit scope, and really focus on what's important. So the concept of thinking about tests first at the other levels of the pyramid transfers really well. The mechanics of writing tests first, however, don't.

I wouldn't, for example, recommend TDDing your UI tests. Doing test first on UI tests is one of those things that sounds good on paper yet turns out not to work so well in practice.

For one, you've got the fact that the UI, at least in the early stages of development, is always changing. So trying to write UI tests against a changing UI is like trying to hit a moving target. Not very easy and extremely frustrating.

Then you've got the fact that until the actual UI gets built, your tests can't prove anything. TDD is about feedback. And these kinds of tests don't give you any. They aren't built for it. Same goes for integration tests.

So as testers, keep the TDD mindset around when you are thinking about adding new features, and certainly begin with the end in mind, as Steven Covey would say in *The 7 Habits of Highly Effective People [Cov94]*, when writing new tests. But don't sweat the mechanics. Let the UI settle down first. Then add the UI and integration tests after.

ANY OTHER BIG TAKE AWAYS FOR US TESTERS HERE?

Refactoring. Did you see how we refactored the code in that final test case from eight lines down into one? You need to do the same things when you're writing code for your tests too. Always look for ways to remove duplication and keep your tests clean.

BY WRITING ALL THESE TESTS IN THE CODE, IS THERE ANY CHANCE NONE OF THIS CONNECTS WHEN WE HOOK IT UP TO THE UI ?

Yes! Good point. TDD gives us really good feedback in the code around whether our design at that level is working, but we always want to hook it up as soon as possible to something that goes end-to-end to see that everything is working.

Because you are right. The way we need to interact with the UI or web services may change how we do things down below. So yes. Start things off with some unit tests, and think about how the data will be reaching your code. But then quickly prove it out end-to-end shortly thereafter.

ARE THERE ANY PLACES WHERE TDD DOESN'T REALLY WORK ?

Yes, there are a few. Anything that is non-deterministic or random is hard to test. It's hard to test the shuffle algorithm on a deck of cards or for a thousand songs in a user's playlist, for example.

Multi-threaded code is hard to test. But in these instances, breaking functionality into smaller, more testable pieces is usually your best approach here. And then bringing it together and testing it the old-fashioned way when you need to make sure it all hangs together.

What We've Learned So Far

Well done, amigo. You made it. You slogged through the building of an RPN style calculator, and you got to experience what it feels like to write tests first. The only thing holding you back now is practice. Lots of practice.

TDD doesn't come naturally to folks. At least not at first. But once you get that you have the ability to create anything you want, and codify it in the form of a test, that's powerful stuff. And this technique will serve you well for all your programming days.

Here's what we saw in this chapter:

- Writing tests first is as much about design as it is about testing.

- You always start with a failing test, and then make it pass and refactor from there.

- TDD is a great place to go to if you're ever feeling stuck and you just want to make something happen one test at a time.

- It's no silver bullet. TDD doesn't magically give you perfect code or wonderful design. You do that. TDD is merely a tool—one of many—to help you get there. Getting there, however, is up to you.

We've only scratched the surface on this huge topic. But if you are interested in learning more, I highly recommend *Test-Driven Development: By Example* [Bec02] by the man who defined it himself, Kent Beck.

Well that's the end of our journey, my friends. A few parting words before you head out into the yonder.

Final Words

Congratulations. You made it!

Certificate of Completion

This certificate is presented to

Your name

For completing a book on

Automated Web Testing

Testers, you now should have the vocabulary, and the beginnings of enough technical skill, to start writing your own automated tests. Congratulations. What you need now is practice. So get out there and look for opportunities to practice what you've learned, and before long you'll be a maestro of automated testing.

Developers. Thank you for reading. None of this automated testing stuff happens without you. So keep giving us the solid base of unit tests all automated testing initiatives require, and continue to help testers with the setup of automated testing environments. There is so much automated testing to be done, it's in your best interests to help out and get everyone going.

And above all, work together. Testing and development clearly go hand in hand. Collaborate with each other, work together, and push the boundaries of this incredible medium of expression that combines art, science, design, and technology.

Anyone can write automated tests. All it takes is some drive, some will, and a little bit of technical know-how. All of which you now possess. So get out there and do it!

Good luck! Till next time.

CSS Cheat Sheet

CSS selectors can be tricky to remember. Here's a quick cheat sheet to help you figure out what the CSS selectors are for page elements you want to interact with in your UI tests.

Grabbing a text box

Google Developer Console
1. Right-click and select Inspect
2. Select Console tab

> $("input[type='text']")

Email CSS Selector

$("input[type='text']")
$("#session_email")
$("input[type='text'][name='session[email]']")
$("input[type='text'][placeholder='Email']")

HTML

```
<input type="text"
       id="session_email"
     name="session[email]"
placeholder="Email">
```

Password CSS Selector

$("input[type='password']")
$("#session_password")
$("input[type='password'][name='session[password]']")
$("input[type='password'][placeholder='Password']")

HTML

```
<input type="password"
        id="session_password"
      name="session[password]"
placeholder="Password">
```

Button CSS Selector

$("button")
$(".btn")
$("button[type=submit]")

HTML

```
<button
class="btn"
type="submit">Sign in</button>
```

Google Chrome Developer Tools

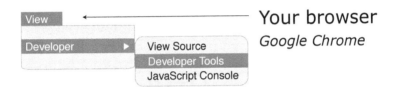

Google Chrome (and other web browsers) have some wonderful tools to help you write your UI and integration tests right from within your browser.

Right-clicking on an HTML page is a quick way to see the underlying HTML. It's useful for seeing all the underlying controls you may need to grab for UI tests.

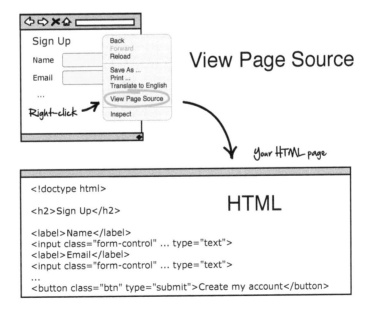

When you find an element you want to grab, right-click it and select Inspect Element or Inspect to see the underlying control.

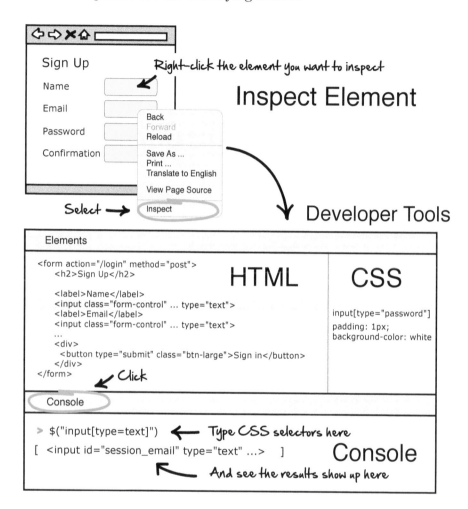

From there, you can then practice writing your CSS selectors to see which page elements you need to grab and use in your tests. See Chapter 2, *Smoking User Interface Tests*, on page 19, for a refresher on how all this works.

Those tools are handy for UI tests. For integration tests, Chrome has your back there too. You can always inspect network traffic if you want to see what kind of HTTP requests are going on when you load a page.

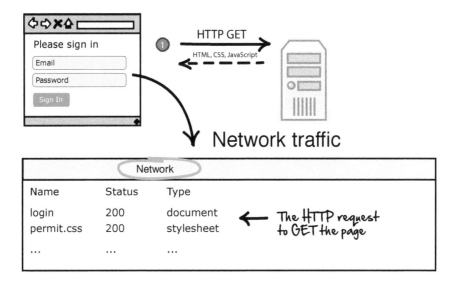

Or if you want to see the results of an HTTP POST.

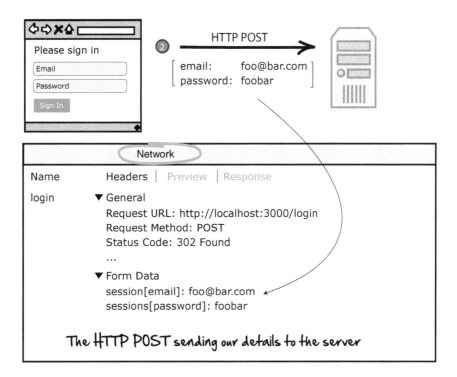

You can see more of how we used these in Chapter 4, *Connecting the Dots with Integration Tests*, on page 53.

Bibliography

[Bec02]   Kent Beck. *Test-Driven Development: By Example*. Addison-Wesley, Boston, MA, 2002.

[Coh09]   Mike Cohn. *Succeeding with Agile: Software Development Using Scrum*. Addison-Wesley, Boston, MA, 2009.

[Cov94]   Stephen R. Covey. *The 7 Habits of Highly Effective People*. The Free Press, New York, NY, 1994.

[Cro08]   Douglas Crockford. *JavaScript: The Good Parts*. O'Reilly & Associates, Inc., Sebastopol, CA, 2008.

[FBBO99]   Martin Fowler, Kent Beck, John Brant, William Opdyke, and Don Roberts. *Refactoring: Improving the Design of Existing Code*. Addison-Wesley, Boston, MA, 1999.

[Hen13]   Elisabeth Hendrickson. *Explore It!*. The Pragmatic Bookshelf, Raleigh, NC, 2013.

[Sub16]   Venkat Subramaniam. *Test-Driving JavaScript Applications*. The Pragmatic Bookshelf, Raleigh, NC, 2016.

Index

Explore Testing and Cucumber

Explore the uncharted waters of exploratory testing and beef up your automated testing with more Cucumber—now for Java, too.

Explore It!

Uncover surprises, risks, and potentially serious bugs with exploratory testing. Rather than designing all tests in advance, explorers design and execute small, rapid experiments, using what they learned from the last little experiment to inform the next. Learn essential skills of a master explorer, including how to analyze software to discover key points of vulnerability, how to design experiments on the fly, how to hone your observation skills, and how to focus your efforts.

Elisabeth Hendrickson
(186 pages) ISBN: 9781937785024. $29
https://pragprog.com/book/ehxta

The Cucumber for Java Book

Teams working on the JVM can now say goodbye forever to misunderstood requirements, tedious manual acceptance tests, and out-of-date documentation. Cucumber—the popular, open-source tool that helps teams communicate more effectively with their customers—now has a Java version, and our bestselling *Cucumber Book* has been updated to match. *The Cucumber for Java Book* has the same great advice about how to deliver rock-solid applications collaboratively, but with all code completely rewritten in Java. New chapters cover features unique to the Java version of Cucumber, and reflect insights from the Cucumber team since the original book was published.

Seb Rose, Matt Wynne & Aslak Hellesoy
(338 pages) ISBN: 9781941222294. $36
https://pragprog.com/book/srjcuc

Secure and Better JavaScript

Secure your Node applications and make writing JavaScript easier and more productive.

Secure Your Node.js Web Application

Cyber-criminals have your web applications in their crosshairs. They search for and exploit common security mistakes in your web application to steal user data. Learn how you can secure your Node.js applications, database and web server to avoid these security holes. Discover the primary attack vectors against web applications, and implement security best practices and effective countermeasures. Coding securely will make you a stronger web developer and analyst, and you'll protect your users.

Karl Düüna
(230 pages) ISBN: 9781680500851. $36
https://pragprog.com/book/kdnodesec

CoffeeScript

Over the last five years, CoffeeScript has taken the web development world by storm. With the humble motto "It's just JavaScript," CoffeeScript provides all the power of the JavaScript language in a friendly and elegant package. This extensively revised and updated new edition includes an all-new project to demonstrate CoffeeScript in action, both in the browser and on a Node.js server. There's no faster way to learn to write a modern web application.

Trevor Burnham
(124 pages) ISBN: 9781941222263. $29
https://pragprog.com/book/tbcoffee2

The Modern Web

Get up to speed on the latest HTML, CSS, and JavaScript techniques.

HTML5 and CSS3 (2nd edition)

HTML5 and CSS3 are more than just buzzwords – they're the foundation for today's web applications. This book gets you up to speed on the HTML5 elements and CSS3 features you can use right now in your current projects, with backwards compatible solutions that ensure that you don't leave users of older browsers behind. This new edition covers even more new features, including CSS animations, IndexedDB, and client-side validations.

Brian P. Hogan
(314 pages) ISBN: 9781937785598. $38
https://pragprog.com/book/bhh52e

Async JavaScript

With the advent of HTML5, front-end MVC, and Node.js, JavaScript is ubiquitous—and still messy. This book will give you a solid foundation for managing async tasks without losing your sanity in a tangle of callbacks. It's a fast-paced guide to the most essential techniques for dealing with async behavior, including PubSub, evented models, and Promises. With these tricks up your sleeve, you'll be better prepared to manage the complexity of large web apps and deliver responsive code.

Trevor Burnham
(104 pages) ISBN: 9781937785277. $17
https://pragprog.com/book/tbajs

The Pragmatic Bookshelf

The Pragmatic Bookshelf features books written by developers for developers. The titles continue the well-known Pragmatic Programmer style and continue to garner awards and rave reviews. As development gets more and more difficult, the Pragmatic Programmers will be there with more titles and products to help you stay on top of your game.

Visit Us Online

This Book's Home Page
https://pragprog.com/book/jrtest
Source code from this book, errata, and other resources. Come give us feedback, too!

Register for Updates
https://pragprog.com/updates
Be notified when updates and new books become available.

Join the Community
https://pragprog.com/community
Read our weblogs, join our online discussions, participate in our mailing list, interact with our wiki, and benefit from the experience of other Pragmatic Programmers.

New and Noteworthy
https://pragprog.com/news
Check out the latest pragmatic developments, new titles and other offerings.

Save on the eBook

Save on the eBook versions of this title. Owning the paper version of this book entitles you to purchase the electronic versions at a terrific discount.

PDFs are great for carrying around on your laptop—they are hyperlinked, have color, and are fully searchable. Most titles are also available for the iPhone and iPod touch, Amazon Kindle, and other popular e-book readers.

Buy now at *https://pragprog.com/coupon*

Contact Us

Online Orders:	*https://pragprog.com/catalog*
Customer Service:	*support@pragprog.com*
International Rights:	*translations@pragprog.com*
Academic Use:	*academic@pragprog.com*
Write for Us:	*http://write-for-us.pragprog.com*
Or Call:	+1 800-699-7764

Milton Keynes UK
Ingram Content Group UK Ltd.
UKHW050936260724
446103UK00003B/23